CARTOGRAPHIES

'. . . explores the co-mappings of bodies and spaces, showcases new perspectives and new visions within the humanities and the arts that testify to the fertility and productivity of new intellectual ventures and explorations.' ***Elizabeth Grosz***

'Even circular maps of the world have blank spots which we prefer to dismiss as the haunts of monsters and other unclassifiable entities rather than beings with whom we must form a relationship or conduct a dialogue. Bodies themselves, the traditional bedrock of material reality, may be the most alien of dragons lurking on the edges of our known world.

With the upheavals and questioning of the Bicentenary and before we are launched into premature celebration of our supposed autonomy through Federation, cartographies and new ways of mapping are in the air. Such enterprises, as these varied essays reveal, explore our exclusions in the very predications upon which our maps and taxonomies are based, outcast elements whose seismic movements disrupt the foundations of our continent.' ***Sneja Gunew***

'Bodies, borders, spaces: this collection is an experiment in the mapping of social experience. Questioning the history of the zoning laws we embody in everyday life, these essays explore some strange, familiar spaces—pragmatist utopia, photographic desire, corporate folk-tale, Aboriginal painting in "translation", Disney World's EPCOT Center—in a world where genetics and medical image technology fabricate "life itself".

By examining the reality of fictions now so active in our lives, *Cartographies* itself creates a space where poststructuralist thinking can work in radical involvement with contemporary cultural politics.' ***Meaghan Morris***

Books of related interest

FEMININE/MASCULINE AND REPRESENTATION
Edited by Terry Threadgold and Anne Cranny-Francis

SEXUAL SUBVERSIONS
Three French feminists
Elizabeth Grosz

BUREAUCRATS, TECHNOCRATS, FEMOCRATS
Anna Yeatman

LAW AND THE SEXES
Ngaire Naffine

PLAYING THE STATE
Australian feminist interventions
Edited by Sophie Watson

SAME DIFFERENCE
Feminism and sexual difference
Carol Lee Bacchi

Forthcoming

HETEROLOGY AND THE POSTMODERN
Julian Pefanis

JACQUES LACAN
A feminist introduction
Elizabeth Grosz

JUDGEMENT OF PARIS
Kevin Murray

STRIKING CHORDS
Sneja Gunew and Kateryna Olijnyk Arthur

CARTOGRAPHIES

Poststructuralism and the mapping of bodies and spaces

edited by
Rosalyn Diprose and Robyn Ferrell

ALLEN & UNWIN

First published in 1991
Allen & Unwin Australia Pty Ltd
8 Napier Street, North Sydney, NSW 2059, Australia

National Library of Australia
Cataloguing-in-publication entry:

Cartographies: poststructuralism and the mapping of bodies and spaces.

Bibliography.
Includes index.
ISBN 0 04 442291 1.

1. Criticism. 2. Structuralism (Literary analysis). 3. Representation (Philosophy). 4. Body, Human (Philosophy). I. Diprose, Rosalyn. II. Ferrell, Robyn.

801.95

Library of Congress Catalog Card No: 90-55744

Cover design: Clea Gazzard
Set in 10/11pt Sabon by Graphicraft Typesetters Ltd, Hong Kong
Printed by Kin Keong Printing, Singapore

Contents

Acknowledgements

Earlier versions of some papers were presented at the *Cartographies* conference at the University of New South Wales in November 1989. We gratefully acknowledge the financial assistance of the Arts Faculty and the School of Philosophy in the running of that conference and in the preparation of this book. Our thanks to Genevieve Lloyd and Venus Kringas in the School of Philosophy, and Rhonda Black and Karen Ward at Allen & Unwin, for advice and support.

Thanks also to Kate Gilroy, Lisa Trahair and Alan Rumsey for their assistance with the preparation of the manuscript, and to Penelope Deutscher and Sarah Redshaw for help with the conference organisation.

The cover is based on a design by Cathryn Vasseleu and Kate Gilroy. We acknowledge John Fairfax Group Pty Ltd for permission to reproduce the photographs on page 122.

Introduction

> You can define a net in one of two ways, depending on your point of view. Normally, you would say that it is a meshed instrument designed to catch fish. But you could, with no great injury to logic, reverse the image and define a net as a jocular lexicographer once did: he called it a collection of holes tied together with string.
>
> Julian Barnes *Flaubert's Parrot*[1]

As a 'meshed instrument', the net as metaphor is required to catch the details of what is to be interpreted, which is to say, what is to be reconstructed. But in the lexicographer's folly, it is the hole, and not the string, that dictates what that object comes to be—by what is allowed to get away.

The merit of the metaphor lies in the implication that language does not simply describe what is. It is rather that the strings of meaning produce the holes in the material world in such a way that what is represented is as much a product of the unsaid as of the said.

Within the metaphor of the net, the object of any discourse is therefore a fabrication. But there is a danger in the way this metaphor reduces truth so summarily to a set of fictions or, at best, to approximations about a real 'out' there' to be hauled in. Somewhere in that briny picture lurks the assumption that the net is thrown over already existing meanings and that the truth of the matter could be caught if only the strings were pulled tight enough. Or, failing that, that all that can be caught is a selection or interpretation.

On the status of a reality outside of our interpretations, Samuel Weber notes that, 'The future of the humanities may well depend on the capacity of . . . society . . . to admit and accept the fictionality of what it assumes to be real, as well as the reality of its fictions'.[2] The first part of Weber's insight seems to have been much more readily accepted than the second in the area of postmodernism and post-structuralist scholarship which has become so fashionable (in the United States, in particular). Perhaps this owes something to the nurture of this kind of theory within disciplines whose object of inquiry is broadly representation—within, that is, fine art, visual art, literary theory and semiotics.[3] It is not to discredit this emphasis, but to restore its radicalism, that the questioning in the following papers is pursued.

Like a net, a map does not simply describe what is. A map does not only set up a grid which determines what can be found by selection or omission. Nor is it merely a series of lines inscribed on a previously blank surface. There is an alterity which provokes the desire to map, to contain and to represent—which is to say, to make familiar. At the same time, the very mapping of this difference produces its differences in terms of the economy of the same. The political reality of the changing map of the world, its allegiances, exclusions and oppression, is testament to cartography as a relevant metaphor. Mapping, as representation, is inextricably caught up in the material production of what it represents.

In the metaphor of cartography, to draw a line is to produce a space, and the production of the space effects the line. The map describes a territory as the compass describes an arc; the lines on the map produce borders beyond which things are seen to be different. Yet the difference of the 'outside' also defines what is 'inside' the border. It is in this sense that our title speaks of the mapping of bodies and spaces, in that much of this collection is preoccupied with how this production of differences takes effect materially.

To speak of the real effects of representation should not produce a collapse of the distinction. On the contrary, a deconstruction of the habit of argument that opposes the real world to our representations of it should, by rights, persuade us of the productive effect of that opposition. For every opposition, produced in discourse, is to that extent produced in the object it describes. Ironically, the proof of this analysis is in the incompleteness of that production, the disturbance that manifests in the borderline cases, the marginal interests and symptomatic exclusions. It is the realisation that something real remains to be represented that persuades us that there is a production at work, even in the most self-evident facts about the world.

This collection begins with an explicit critique of the conservatism of some post-structural interventions into theories of representation in Anglo-American scholarship. Richard Rorty's failure to take account of the materiality of representation is the specific target of

Robyn Ferrell's chapter, and it is Rorty's pragmatism, governed by a democratic equivalence, that Ferrell locates as the source of Rorty's failure.

Geoffrey Batchen and Jennifer Biddle explore manifestations of the desire to map and contain difference, and the particular effects of that desire. Batchen interrogates the desire to photograph, locating it beyond the invention of photography and arguing that it arose within and contributed to a wider modification of subject and object. Jennifer Biddle explores the desire to map cultural difference in an analysis of the uncertain effects of translation in the dissemination of Aboriginal art.

The different ways in which the production of bodies take effect materially are explored in the second part of this collection. Paul Patton highlights a neglected aspect of philosophy—the philosopher's body, which he argues is a productive site. Through Nietzsche, Patton rethinks the relation between power and bodies to allow for the production of new bodies within contemporary social spaces.

The political import of post-structuralist interventions has been lost partly because they have left the sciences untouched. Despite the interrogation of the activities of science, the assumption persists that scientific modes of representation are not constitutive of their objects, as the representations of the humanities are. Cathryn Vasseleu looks at the constitutive role of metaphor in the life sciences, in particular in the models and images deployed in medical imaging technology. Rosalyn Diprose argues that modern genetics does not merely make sense of bodily differences but is implicated in producing those differences, through the ways it represents itself and its object. In this, Diprose reveals the theory of genetics, and not merely its application, to be a question of ethics.

The chapters in part three explore the unacknowledged effects of the representation of sexual difference within an economy that can only deal in the same. Moira Gatens argues that the body politic is a representation of a particular kind of male body, at the expense of others. Vicki Kirby examines how 'woman' takes place as the embodiment of essentialisms, in response to the contemporary feminist difficulty in accounting for sexual difference as bodily.

The organising of various visual and spatial fields is explored in the final part of the collection. Steven Rugare finds a mapping of American identity, and an attendant effacement of cultural differences, in the apparently benign architectural arrangement of Disney World's EPCOT Center. Helen Grace observes the production of a new kind of masculinity in the image of the corporate hero/villain on the business pages of the newspaper.

Photography, architecture, art, anthropology, political institutions, financial activities and scientific practices all receive attention in this collection. The exploration of the production of borders, and the bodies and spaces they effect, is necessarily a trans-disciplinary project. Some of these papers were first presented as part of an interdisciplinary conference held in the Arts Faculty at the University of New South Wales in 1989. As opportunities for interdisciplinary studies increase in universities, traditional boundaries between disciplines, and more broadly between the sciences and the humanities, are put at issue.[4] The opportunity is presented to scrutinise the process of production of the university itself, its disciplines and its knowledge. It is hoped that this collection can play its part in that scrutiny.

Rosalyn Diprose
Robyn Ferrell

PART I
The Mapping

ROBYN FERRELL

1 Richard Rorty and the poet's utopia

Richard Rorty's vision of the liberal utopia, which he outlines in the introduction to his recent book, *Contingency, Irony and Solidarity*,[1] is an explicit example of a narrative that is common, if submerged, in many recent adaptations of post-structuralism. The utopian pleasures of the text promise liberation from the cramping empiricism of science, the leaden labour of politics, and the dragging chains of metaphysics. Or is it a delusional escape? Rorty's book is dedicated: 'In memory of six liberals: my parents and grandparents'. This chapter dedicates itself to exploring the strange coupling of liberalism and post-structuralism.

Rorty writes a contemporary kind of pragmatism which makes use of post-structuralist writing against the scientism of Anglo-American philosophy.[2] He has popularised a particular reading of philosopy as 'just a kind of writing' in American philosophical and literary circles. However, the problem for Rorty is that while he wants to challenge scientism with a Vision Splendid of the literary imagination, he does not want to question the liberal subject on whose behalf he writes.

Rorty does not see the need for a theory of subject-making, a theory of the production of meaning/value nor a critique of inequality (all significant preoccupations in French post-structuralism). He refers to these kinds of questions as 'not theoretical'.[3] But they are not beyond theory, as he implies; he *already has* a theory of them, the pragmatist/liberal postulations for which he does not argue.

Rorty's pragmatism is aestheticised. Speech act theorists like John Searle give us a straight 'mercantile' pragmatism in their conception of the use-value of language as a currency of intention. The result for Searle is that metaphor, fiction and other literary uses of language appear as ancillary to, or as deviations from, 'ordinary language'. His analysis of fictional discourse then 'leaves one crucial question unanswered', as Searle himself admits: 'Why bother? That is, why do we attach such importance and effort to texts which contain largely pretended speech acts?' Since Searle's theory already presupposes that use-value is a product of successful communication of intentions, it is not surprising that this importance can't be accounted for on the theory.[4] Rorty's view, on the other hand, emphasises the use-value of poetic language. Whereas for Searle the end product is to be communication of intentions, for Rorty it is the creation of individuality. Liberal individualism meets the Nietzschean self-creation as a work of art.

But the individual of liberalism is a unit of equivalence in the free-market society: 'All men are equal'. The currency for exchange of these units is their freedom, which they are given in equal measure at the start of the game. The guarantee of their equivalence is their solidarity, the brotherhood that ensures that individualism will not result in conflicts of interest that cannot be resolved by appeal to their similarity.[5] 'Liberty Equality Fraternity' succinctly abbreviates it.

Within this individualism that is paradoxically an equivalence, Rorty cannot succeed in claiming the space he wants for a Nietzschean 'strong poet'. No pragmatist labour can release itself from the *levelling of meaning* that results from this equivalence: the liberal individual cannot differ in any significant sense from his brother. Representing all terms as theoretically equivalent rules out a theoretical account of how meaning is produced. Meaning will become, by default, a string of contingencies and accidents of definition, a view Rorty may not be uncomfortable with. However, it would put him at odds with the French tradition he borrows from, which takes seriously Lacan's marriage of Saussure and Freud. 'Every subject is a signifier for another subject', subjectivity is a formation 'like a language' in that it gains its value *in its difference from other subjects/signifiers*.

Rorty does not escape the supplementary nature of the literary and poetic either, because he must serve the opposition of public to private on which the liberal subject relies. The private self is always supplementary to this subject, from the moment he is postulated as springing, ready-made, to the defence of his freedom in consensus with other citizens like him. The liberal individual is not his childhood, hunger, nor his desire; these states of being do not define him. He is first and foremost an agent,[6] able to contract with others on the basis of his rational self-interest.

DICHOTOMIES

Despite an acquaintance with Derrida,[7] familiar dichotomies uphold Rorty's sanguine prose: public/private, real/representation, subject/object, philosopher/poet.

> Authors like Kierkegaard, Nietzsche, Baudelaire, Proust, Heidegger and Nabokov are useful as exemplars, as illustrations of what private perfection—a self-created, autonomous, human life—can be like. Authors such as Marx, Mill, Dewey, Habermas and Rawls are fellow citizens rather than exemplars. They are engaged in a shared, social effort—the effort to make our institutions and practices more just and less cruel. We shall only think of these two kinds of writers as *opposed* if we think that a more comprehensive philosophical outlook would let us hold self-creation and justice, private perfection and human solidarity, in a single vision . . . There is no way in which philosophy, or any other theoretical discipline, will ever let us do that. The closest we will come to joining these two quests is to see the aim of a just and free society as letting its citizens be as privatistic, 'irrationalist', and aestheticist as they please so long as they do it on their own time—causing no harm to others and using no resources needed by those less advantaged.[8]

Rorty establishes his public/private distinction by dividing into two groups a selection of writers who differ, and by characterising their theoretical differences as the difference between the public and the private. This difference is then taken for a 'familiar standoff' that philosophy has tried in vain to resolve. It is suggested that to see the views of these writers as opposed is to be involved in a metaphysical search for unity; but this project cannot be achieved. Rorty therefore concludes that the only outcome is to reject the view that they oppose each other, and to reconcile them in a liberal pluralism such as he will go on to describe.

Rorty considers that the public and the private only seem opposed because we insist on viewing them in relation to each other. He recommends we insulate them from each other: 'This book tries to show how things look if we drop the demand for a theory which unifies the public and private, and are content to treat the demands of self-creation and of human solidarity as equally valid, yet forever incommensurable.'[9] However, the public/private distinction is all about the commensurable. *It is a relation.* To refuse to acknowledge that public and private are opposed is to ignore that what is produced by the distinction is an opposition.

Ironically, this insulation makes them precisely commensurable. Reduced to the status of 'vocabularies', they are part of a great narrative of equivalence, the analogue of the liberal individual itself. The differences between these writers, far from having been preserved in this maneouvre, are obliterated. For one equals the other, and they differ only in their detail.

The possibility of there being a theoretical move that elucidates the entanglement of the private in the public is ruled out. The private is that which happens 'on your own time', that is, in private, so Rorty's reconciliation is conservative in character, in the sense of being reconciled to the dichotomy.

This reconciliation prepares the ground for the utopia. Rorty then sketches the figure of the 'liberal ironist', whose utopia it is. A liberal is a person who thinks 'that cruelty is the worst thing we do'; an ironist a person 'who faces up to the contingency of his or her most central beliefs and desires—someone sufficiently historicist and nominalist to have abandoned the idea that those central beliefs and desires refer back to something beyond the reach of time and chance.'

Which of us is not such a liberal in our waking lives? The ironist, too; are there any of the philosophically initiated who imagine their beliefs and desires are written in the stars, beyond the reach of time and chance? But our assent turns out to commit us to a stronger relativism; to the position that these desires are therefore ungroundable. 'Liberal ironists are people who include among these ungroundable desires their own hope that suffering will be diminished . . .'[10] And yet those desires are strictly grounded in the text of experience, in the body whose experience it is. The move which has committed us to recognising our desires as ungroundable rests on opposing contingency to necessity in time-honoured metaphysical fashion.

If desire cannot be grounded 'beyond time and chance', this does not make it groundless; and the appearance that it does is an effect achieved by representing it within the logic of the opposition. The liberal ironist, reconciled to the private as 'on one's own time', and accepting that the contingent is ungroundable, has merely agreed to abide by the very oppositions that produce the contradictions he now accepts as fate.

> But if we could ever become reconciled to the idea that most of reality is indifferent to our descriptions of it, and that the human self is created by the use of a vocabulary rather than being adequately or inadequately expressed in a vocabulary, then we should at last have assimilated what was true in the Romantic idea that truth is made rather than found.[11]

Another reconciliation to another opposition: that between 'reality' and 'our descriptions of it'. To the liberal ironist, reality remains indifferent to descriptions, but the self is made by them. The self creates itself, romantically, in the freedom of an existence prior to essence.

Is the liberal ironist a post-structuralist? Not quite. The liberal ironist's self is equated with consciousness and with a mentality whose embodiment is theoretically insignificant. This is a liberal necessity; if the self is to be a unit of exchange, then each self must be in principle the same. Rorty reads Freud as a theory of mind, not of psyche. According to Rorty,

> Freud gave up Plato's attempt to bring together the public and the private, the parts of the state and the parts of the soul . . . He distinguishes sharply between a private ethic of self-creation and a public ethic of mutual accommodation. He persuades us that there is no bridge between them provided by universally shared beliefs or desires . . . In Freud's account, our conscious private goals are as idiosyncratic as the unconscious obsessions and phobias from which they have branched off.[12]

The move from 'universally shared desires' to 'idiosyncratic goals' overlooks Freud's meticulous modelling of the individual in society. The hysterical symptom, for example, is a compromise between individual desire and social requirement, that is, it represents a sexual desire to which society must refuse direct expression. While desires, beliefs and symptoms are particular to the subject and her history, they are not therefore idiosyncratic or peculiar to her, since their structuring is governed by social norms at work in her individual circumstances.

The body of this self is a contingent detail, not a defining surface; neither the body/unconscious, nor the repression that founds it, are represented in Rorty's reading of Freud. As such, the real is insulated from representation in a way reminiscent of the insulation of the public from the private; the self remains an ideational process, negotiated parallel to an 'out there' which is material, the indifferent reality.

But what of Freud's little boy, wrestling with the Oedipus complex, grasping that the sight of the genitals of his sister represents a cultural imperative? This sign, her lack, is both flesh and representation—and his own flesh is threatened with castration if he doesn't learn this sign. A relationship of greater entailment between the real and the representational is proposed in post-structuralist accounts of the production of experience of the real in representations of it. A representation of the woman's genitals as lacking something produces the reality of sexual difference, which is 'indifferent' only in the sense that it is resistant to our denials of it.[13] But the liberal ironist, while he accepts the unproblematic distinction between real and representational, meets with a frustrating 'ungroundability': 'The difficulty faced by a philosopher who, like myself, is sympathetic . . . is to avoid hinting that this suggestion gets something right, that my sort of philosophy corresponds to the way things really are'.[14] To what, then, does it correspond? But the liberal ironist cannot leap the gap, the gap opened up in insulating the real from the representational. How can his philosophy reach beyond representation to 'the way things really are', while these two terms are defined in opposition to each other?

Languages and signs are human, but this does not make them the product of human agency. The word is subordinate to the system of relations which define it in language, and the subject is subordinate to the system of relations that she finds in her cultural scope. She can take no credit for authorship of truth, which is why to speak of truth as 'made' and not 'found' is also misleading—the made/found opposition, imbued with human agency, is a consequence of the opposition of self to reality.

Instead of speaking of the self as creating itself in the choice of vocabularies, Foucault, Derrida and Lacan posit the subject as inheriting the burden of a speaking position incarnated in history. If the ironist must accept anything in the name of contingency it may be that *nevertheless the beliefs and desires are grounded*. But this acceptance must compromise the opposing of contingent to necessary. The appearance of choice between truth in the world or truth in language is an after-effect of the distinction having been made.

OFF-CAMERA

The view that the contingent nature of truth leads to a set of choices suitable for self-creation is a popular reading since its outcome is in harmony with the liberal goal of freedom. However, the preservation of dichotomies by denying their operation leads to a repression of features that, were they displayed, might be seen to compromise that freedom.

I have argued that, despite his use of post-structuralism, Rorty separates that which is real from that which represents it in language and theory, that which is public from that which is private, that which is necessary from that which is contingent on the basis of familiar oppositions. He then disguises their opposition by insulating them from each other. So, the private goes on 'on one's own time', the contingent is ungroundable, and reality is indifferent to our descriptions of it. The result, then, is that the opposition *as a discursive function* is repressed.

What is the effect of this? Representation, which for Rorty is synonymous with language, remains supplementary to the central real of liberal society, but this is simultaneously obscured since *this real is missing*. It is this which produces the effect of choice. On the face of the text, nothing bears the weight of the production of meaning and value; this is because the scene of production of the liberal subject is elsewhere, off-stage, in the economic model of a free market in which competition among equals produces value of all kinds. This is the real; seemingly absent, but merely out of the picture. Representation (language) can then perform its supplementary dance of free-play, self-expression and idiosyncrasy, while the theoretical burden of value production is taken elsewhere, in the real of the free market.

The failures of this choice view of self-creation are grounded in the frauds of a free market philosophy. But the liberal ironist shows us only a detail of a bigger picture—and not the most important part of it. Language is not important for Rorty, despite the fact that he writes of little else, because it carries nothing of the structural weight of a society: it is not a load-bearing structure.[15]

This gives Rorty's theory of language and 'philosophy as a kind of writing' the magical effect: no visible means of support. But it also creates a problem for it; how to account for change in a changeable world? Rorty's attempts to portray it as a choice of vocabularies reduce the history of ideas to a marketing exercise (which indeed exposes the free-market in play behind it):

> The method is to redescribe lots and lots of things in new ways, until you have created a pattern of linguistic behaviour which will tempt the rising generation to adopt it, thereby causing them to look for appropriate new forms of non-linguistic behavior ...[16]

The liberal ironist then relies on a humanist moralism to prevent the contingent from becoming the arbitrary, ergo, the capricious:

> In subsequent chapters, I shall try to show how a recognition of that contingency leads to a recognition of the contingency of conscience, and how both recognitions lead to a picture of intellectual and moral progress as a history of increasingly useful metaphors rather than of increasing understanding of how things really are.[17]

The proposal of a use-value for metaphor is not supported by an account of what metaphor is useful *for*, and similarly a recourse to an idea of progress begs the question. In effect, the fixity and unity of a necessity beyond time and chance is replaced by a contingency of progress and utility, but the reversal is merely apparent. The opposition of 'increasingly useful metaphors' to 'increasing understanding of how things really are' belies their similarity. But both are narratives ascribing coherence through a unifying principle: in the latter an external reality, in the former the purposes/desires of the subject. With the postulation of progress a unity is upheld. That unity, however much it professes a more general freedom, is the image of the liberal ironist and his free market purposes.

> One of my aims in this book is to suggest the possibility of a liberal utopia; one in which ironism, in the relevant sense, is universal. A post-

> metaphysical culture seems to me no more impossible than a postreligious one, and equally desirable ...[18]

This utopia is realisable and human solidarity is to be the goal:

> It is to be achieved not by inquiry but by imagination, the imaginative ability to see strange people as fellow sufferers ... Solidarity is not discovered by reflection but created. It is created by increasing our sensitivity to the particular details of the pain and humiliation of other, unfamiliar sorts of people. Such increased sensitivity makes it more difficult to marginalize people different from ourselves ...[19]

The original gesture, which removed conflict from between the two groups of writers, will be repeated by the citizen, who will come to see all of us, however strange, as equivalent. Our difference will not matter. The liberal identifies the cause of cruelty as the lack of imagination. The possibility of real conflict of interest has lost its structural burden, and is now only ascribable to contingent failures of imagination.

Despite the apparent altruism, this is a dubious ethics. Grounded in narcissism, it makes the other's survival dependent on his ability to be like me.[20] As such, it is a symptom of the psychopathology of imperialism.

UTOPIAN DESIRES

Rorty anticipates a utopian turn against theory and toward narrative. He commends ethnography and journalism, as well as the novel, as genres that are specifically 'not-theory' in the liberating sense.

Freud has made every man a poet, and in the liberal utopia each will explore his private vocabularies for the adornment of his individualism:

> For Freud, nobody is dull through and through, for there is no such thing as a dull unconscious. What makes Freud more useful and more plausible than Nietzsche is that he does not relegate the vast majority of humanity to the status of dying animals. For Freud's account of unconscious fantasy shows us how to see every human life as a poem ...[21]

Freud is one of a company who, in the 'spirit of playfulness and irony', has already begun the utopia:

> For it somehow became possible, toward the end of the nineteenth century, to take the activity of redescription more lightly than it had ever been taken before. It became possible to juggle several descriptions of the same event without asking which one was right—to see redescription as a tool rather than a claim to have discovered essence. It thereby became possible to see a new vocabulary not as something which was supposed to replace

> all other vocabularies, something which claimed to represent reality, but simply as one more vocabulary, one more human project, one person's chosen metaphoric.[22]

'It somehow became possible'; this miracle is quickly revealed to be a sleight of hand, making it possible to juggle. The juggling avoids having to ask which one is right, that is, it avoids the anxiety of conflicting claims to truth. Which, through and through, is the liberal ironist's great anxiety; conflict is his greatest fear. He has already determined how to resolve it; by declaring all to be like him and therefore to share his interests.

The liberal ironist, having thus committed himself to the postulation of every subject as equivalent, to eradicate this anxiety need now only dispense with the universal in favour of the particular. The possibility that *there are different speaking materialities from which different and conflicting truth emerges* cannot on the theory be entertained. 'Insofar as one can attribute philosophical views to Freud, one can say that he is as much a pragmatist as James and as much a perspectivalist as Nietzsche'...[23] Pragmatism has consistently failed to read that perspectivalism as implying conflict, whereas post-structuralist readings of Nietzsche make it a logical implication, since the self must create itself by excluding the other.[24] Freud bases the possibility of society on the individual's sacrifice of Oedipal desire, arguably the founding lesson in conflicts of interest.

The liberal ironist, then, is involved in a disavowal when he invokes perspectivalism without a clash of perspectives. However, the conflict between 'speaking materialities' (which refers not only to the positions from which we speak but the way we are spoken in them) cannot be abolished by fiat. Therefore, since the liberal ironist knows 'the power of language to make new and different things possible and important', he must be on guard against the return of the repressed, those other interests he has sought to obscure. For what if other interests were to be spoken and heard? It becomes imperative to depreciate the significance of these self-actualising vocabularies, and to seal off attempts to take them seriously as corresponding with reality or having claims on truth. This must be the import of the banishment of theory in favour of narrative in the 'postmetaphysical' utopia.

The implication is that we are constrained by theory, in its oppressive custody and that our release from this is an emancipation devoutly to be wished. Derrida's critique of western metaphysics becomes read as this kind of liberation. But the rest of Derrida, the *différance* which prevents any liberation from being complete, this is a *remainder* for which the liberal ironist cannot see a use.[25] Its effects must be left out of account, just as significant features of Freud's account must be ignored to arrive at the delightful poetic pleasure he anticipates.

And this is where that well-worn opposition between philosophy and literature will be called to play its part. In the romantic view of language in this poet's utopia, a powerful desire is satisfied. The defence against conflict is entrenched, and the *desire* that promotes literature as an escape takes its revenge on philosophy and the Platonic jailer. This is the phantasmagorical satisfaction of the liberal utopia.

The utopia is to be 'an endless proliferating realization of Freedom, rather than a convergence toward an already existing Truth'. And yet, without the disturbing insistence of a remainder, what keeps these narratives proliferating, and in response to what? *Différance* returns, in the manner of the repressed, to disturb the peace of the liberal utopia.

Has the liberal ironist paid too high a price for the repression of conflict and contradiction? In exchange for equality/equivalence between speaking positions, he has surrendered language as 'something that represents reality', and so as anything that could have significance. It is utopian to picture a society where conflict and contradiction is ruled out. But the irony is that the strong poet cannot write in it. The poet's utopia is characterised finally by a deafening silence. For why listen? What is to be said? Sad strong poets of Rorty's imagination; endlessly speaking, having nothing to say.

GEOFFREY BATCHEN

2 Desiring production itself: *Notes on the invention of photography*

'Begin at the beginning,' the King said gravely,
'and go on till you come to the end; then stop.'

The King's advice to Alice, as recounted in Lewis Carroll's *Alice in Wonderland*, has been taken to heart by those who write the history of photography. The end is apparently not yet in sight, but the beginning is in almost every account identified with the invention of a marketable photographic apparatus and the successful production of the first photographs. Not only does this originary event mark the starting point, or at least the first climactic moment, of their narrative structures; it has come to represent the one common empirical incident in an otherwise unruly and quarrelsome ensemble of photographic practices and discourses. For this reason the story of the invention of photography has become the stable platform on which all the medium's many subsequent manifestations are presumed to be founded. (To paraphrase Derrida, photography's historians have a vested interest in moving as quickly as possible from the troubling philosophical question 'What is photography?' to the safe and expository one 'Where and when did photography begin?'[1]) At the same time, the circumstances of photography's invention are commonly used to establish the medium's continuity with a linear development of Western practices of representation reaching back to, inevitably, the Renaissance. Any questioning of photography's beginnings represents therefore a questioning of the trajectory of photography's history as a whole.

It was on 7 January 1839, in the form of a speech by François Arago to the French Academy of Sciences, that the invention of photography was officially announced to the world.[2] Further enthusiastic speeches about Louis Daguerre's amazing image-making process were subsequently made to the Chamber of Deputies on 15 June and finally to a combined meeting of the Academy of Sciences and Fine Arts on 19 August. It was only on this latter date that the daguerreotype and its camera apparatus were actually ready to be introduced to an already eager market. Indeed, so eager was this market that within the space of a few months the daguerreotype had found its way to almost every corner of the globe and infiltrated almost every conceivable genre of image making.

Meanwhile, over in England, William Henry Fox Talbot had been motivated by the news of Daguerre's discovery to hurriedly announce that he had also been conducting some experiments with a photographic process. His process, significantly different from that devised by Daguerre, was subsequently described in detail on 31 January 1839, in the form of a paper delivered to the Royal Society. After undergoing a few technical refinements, Talbot's paper-based image and negative-positive method proved even more amenable than the daguerreotype to a wide variety of uses, and provided the basic principles of the photography we still use today.

So no-one would want to deny that 1839 was an important year in the life of photography, particularly with regard to the direction of its subsequent technical, instrumental and entrepreneurial developments. However the traditional emphasis on 1839, and on the pioneering figures of Daguerre and Talbot, has tended to distract attention from the wider significance of the actual timing of photography's emergence into our culture. This paper aims first to establish this timing and then to briefly articulate something of that significance.

In the introduction to his authoritative tome *The Origins of Photography*, Helmut Gernsheim went so far as to describe the timing of photography's invention as 'the greatest mystery in its history'.

> Considering that knowledge of the chemical as well as the optical principles of photography was fairly widespread following Schulze's experiment (in 1725) ... the circumstance that photography was not invented earlier remains the greatest mystery in its history.... It had apparently never occurred to any of the multitude of artists of the seventeenth and eighteenth centuries who were in the habit of using the camera obscura to try to fix its image permanently ...[3]

Why 1839 and not before? This is the question that continues to haunt the history of photography's invention. But how are the medium's historians to engage with it? More to the point, how are we to develop a *critical*, and from that, a *political* understanding of photography's timing? Some historians have looked to Marxist and psychoanalytic models of historiography in this regard, with limited success. However, in relation to the specific question of photography's origins, perhaps the archaeological methods of French philosopher Michel Foucault may be more helpful. Foucault's various archaeologies have, after all, concerned themselves at least in part with a critique of traditional historical ideas about invention and beginnings.

> Archaeology is not in search of inventions; and it remains unmoved at the moment (a very moving one, I admit) when for the first time someone was sure of some truth; it does not try to restore the light of those joyful mornings. But neither is it concerned with the average phenomena of opinion, with the dull grey of what everyone at a particular period might repeat. What it seeks . . . is not to draw up a list of founding saints; it is to uncover the regularity of a discursive practice.[4]

Following Foucault, we might find it useful to shift the emphasis of our investigation of photography's timing from 1839, and the two founding saints of Daguerre and Talbot, to an earlier moment in the medium's history—to the appearance of a regular discursive practice for which photography is the desired object. The timing of the invention of photography is thereby assumed to coincide with its conceptual and metaphoric rather than its technological or functional manifestations. Accordingly this paper will ask, not 'Who invented photography?' but rather, 'At what moment in history did the discursive *desire* to photograph emerge and begin to insistently manifest itself? At what moment did photography shift from an occasional, isolated, individual fantasy to a demonstrably widespread, social *imperative*?' When, in other words, did evidence of a desire to photograph begin to appear with sufficient regularity and internal consistency to be described in Foucault's terms as a discursive practice?

One historian, Pierre Harmant, has already offered a surprisingly crowded list of 24 people who claimed at one time or another to have been the first to have practiced photography; seven of these came from France, six from England, five from Germany, one from Belgium, one was American, one Spanish, one Norwegian, one Swiss and one a Brazilian. Upon further examination of their claims, Harmant concluded that 'of these, four only had solutions which were truly original'.[5] However this is not a criterion that is particularly pertinent to an investigation of the desire to photograph. It is, after all, the mythopoetic significance of such a discourse that is at issue, rather than the historical accuracy or import of individual texts or claimants. Originality of method, accuracy of chemical formulae, success or failure; these irrelevancies need not be taken into account when compiling a list of names and dates of those who felt a desire to photograph. All that need be deleted from this list are those persons, and there are many of them, who only began their experiments after first hearing of the successes of either Daguerre or Talbot. These missing figures were often important to the future developments of photography as a technology and a practice. However, as far as the emergence of a photo-desire is concerned they represent no more than, as Foucault puts it, 'the dull grey of what everyone at a particular period might repeat'.[6]

Here then is the roll-call, undoubtedly an incomplete and speculative one, of those who recorded or subsequently claimed for themselves the onset of a desire to photograph; Wedgwood (England, c. 1790–1802), Brougham (England, 1794), Davy (England, c. 1800–02), Nicéphore and Claude Niépce (France, 1814), Morse (United States, c. 1821), Daguerre (France, 1824), Hubert (France, c. 1828), Wattles (United States, 1828), Florence (Brazil, 1832), Talbot (England, 1833), Hoffmeister (Germany, 1834), Gerber (Switzerland, 1836), Heath (England, 1837), Bayard (France, c. 1837), Zapetti (Spain, c. 1837), and von Wunsch (Germany/France, 1839).[7]

These are the persons we might call the proto-photographers. As authors and experimenters they produced a voluminous collection of aspirations for which some sort of photography was in each case the desired result. Sometimes this is literally so. We find Niépce writing in 1827 to Daguerre, for example, 'in order to respond to the *desire* which you have been good enough to express' (his emphasis) and find Daguerre replying in the following year that 'I cannot hide the fact that I am burning with desire to see your experiments from nature'.[8] On other occasions we are left to read this desire in the objects they sought to have represented—invariably 'views' (of landscape), nature, and/or the image found in the mirror of the camera obscura—or alternatively in the words and phrases they use to describe their imaginary or still-fledgling processes. Talbot offers a representative example of such a description in his 1839 paper to the Royal Society.

> The most transitory of things, a shadow, the proverbial emblem of all that is fleeting and momentary, may be fettered by the spells of our '*natural magic*', and may be fixed for ever in the position which it seemed only destined for a single instant to occupy.[9]

There is already much that could be said about the choice of these particular objects and words. However it is first worth noting that the writings of the various proto-photographers are by no means the only source available to photographic historians of a discourse of this kind. In the last two decades of the eighteenth century it is also possible to find, for example, increasing evidence of a desire that might be called photographic figured in the fields of literature, philosophy and aesthetic criticism.

As early as 1782, William Gilpin, the English clergyman and famous advocate of picturesque theory, had been moved to express some vexation at not having the means to adequately capture the fleeting visual sensations of his river journey. In his *Observations on the River Wye*, he makes the following comment.

> Many of the objects, which had floated so rapidly past us, if we had had time to examine them, would have given us sublime, and beautiful hints in landscape: some of them seemed even well combined, and ready prepared for the pencil: but in so quick a succession, one blotted out another.[10]

In 1791 we find Gilpin again wishing for the impossible, this time for the ability to make his Claude Glass 'fix' its transient reflected image.

> A succession of high-coloured pictures is continually gliding before the eye. They are like the visions of the imagination; or the brilliant landscapes of a dream. Forms, and colours in brightest array, fleet before us; and if the transient glance of a good composition happen to unite with them, we should give any price to fix and appropriate the scene.[11]

William Cowper addresses himself to a similar problem in his 1785 poem entitled 'The Task'. In the passage below he suggests a solution in which the mind of the poet must become a camera obscura, but one with the entirely imaginary capability of being able to hold fast the transient images that flit across its mirrored surface.

> To arrest the fleeting images that fill
> The mirror of the mind, and hold them fast,
> And force them sit, till he has pencilled off
> A faithful likeness of the forms he views.[12]

Cowper was not the only one to exercise such fantasies. In 1802 the Royal Society was told by Humphry Davy of Tom Wedgwood's interest in the images formed within the camera obscura; Davy insisted that 'to copy these images was the first object of Mr Wedgwood in his researches'.[13] This could equally well have been said of Niépce, Morse, Daguerre, Hubert, Talbot, Wattles, Bayard, Florence and Zapetti, all of whom spoke of wanting to fix the image in their camera obscuras, and to capture 'the vivid image of external nature which it displays'.[14] However such an interest was by no means confined to Gilpin, Cowper and the proto-photographers.

Samuel Taylor Coleridge uses the camera obscura metaphor in 1817 to describe his poetic ideal; 'creation rather than painting, or if painting, yet such, and with such co-presence of the whole picture flash'd at once upon the eye, as the sun paints in a camera obscura'.[15] In the 1820s we find another English poet, John Clare, speaking similarly of 'an instrument . . . which he had fashiond [sic] that was to take landscapes almost by itself'. However, as he tells us, despite his own best efforts the pencil drawings obtained using this instrument were, 'but poor shadows of the original & the sun with its instantaneous sketches made better figures of the objects in their shadows'.[16] The ideal imagined by Coleridge and Clare—an instantaneous sketch made by the sun—was also shared by some painters. In 1833 for example, John Constable published a book on landscape painting in which, he claimed; 'an attempt has been made to arrest the more abrupt and transient appearance of the CHIAR'OSCURO IN NATURE . . . to give "to one brief moment caught from fleeting time" a lasting and sober existence . . .'[17]

It is the frustration as much as the aspiration evidenced in these kinds of remarks—their yearning for the impossible, for the ability to represent a moment in time and space that is simultaneously fixed and transient—which makes them of interest to a history of the desire to photograph. For this is a frustration that is newly arisen, a frustration that is not to be found, at least not quite in this form, amongst painters and poets in earlier decades and centuries.

The discursive desire I have described as photo-prophetic obviously coincides with a quite singular moment in Western history. This point needs to be emphasised; the fact that the desire to photograph only appears as a regular discourse at a particular time and place. The inference clearly is that it was only possible to think 'photography' at this specific historical conjuncture, that photography as a concept has an identifiable historical and cultural specificity. Now it might be argued that there had been a number of earlier instances of this photographic desire, like Schulze's experiments with light-sensitive chemicals which were published in 1727, and Tiphaigne de la Roche's allegorical novel written in 1760. However what is striking about such possible approximations of photography is how few and far between they are until the 1790s. Much more overwhelming in this regard is the vast *absence* of talk about images automatically fixing themselves prior to this period. From a virtual dearth of signs of a desire to photograph, the historical archive reveals the onset only in the last decade of the eighteenth century of a rapidly growing, widely dispersed and increasingly urgent need for that-which-was-to-become-photography. By the 1830s this need, a product of Western culture rather than of some isolated individual genius, was well established amongst an intelligentsia scattered throughout Europe and its colonial outposts (England, USA, France, Belgium, Brazil, Germany, Norway, Spain, Switzerland).

Indeed by 1839 the desire to photograph was apparently so well established that Arago could in that year confidently assume to speak for all when he claimed that 'everyone who has admired these images [produced in a camera obscura] will have felt regret that they could not be rendered permanent'.[18] Later in the same year Arago was again moved to declare that

> there is no one, who, after having observed the nicety of the outlines, the correctness of shape and colour, together with that of the shade and light of the images represented by this instrument, has not greatly regretted that they should not be preserved of *their own accord*; no one that has not ardently desired the discovery of some means to fix them on the focal screen . . .[19]

'There is no one who has not ardently desired some means to fix images of their own accord.' Arago's assumption that this once novel desire is now a universal imperative brings us directly back to the question already posed by the quotation from Gernsheim. Why should the ardent desire that Arago describes have arisen at this particular time, rather than at some prior or subsequent moment in the long history of European uses of the camera obscura, or indeed in the long history of European image making in general? Given that a basic knowledge of the existence of light-sensitive chemicals had been popularly available since the 1720s, why does the discursive desire to photograph only begin to emerge in the 1790s and not before?

It seems a simple, almost trivial, question, and yet this matter of timing is a crucial one as far as the cultural *meaning* of photography is concerned. It is no surprise, then, to find that in recent years a number of eminent photo-historians have sought to provide a satisfactory explanation. Mercifully, few of these historians have centered their explanations on the familiar quest for the medium's first inventor or premier product. Most have instead tried to relate photography's emergence to contemporary developments in other areas of European cultural life. These have included, for example, various developments in art (perspective, realism, modernism), in science (physics, chemistry, mechanisation, instrument making) and/or in social and economic formations (the rising dominance of bourgeois ideology, the demand from this class for portrait images).

Who could deny that each of these areas of development contributed to (or is it that they themselves arose from?) the same conditions of possibility from which photography itself was to emerge? However these explanations still provide only a partial understanding of the actual specificity and meaning of photography's timing. Indeed if one had the space here to investigate each of these explanations in detail, and especially to examine them in relation to the available archive of speculations provided by the proto-photographers, one might well find that the evidence of their influence on the sudden emergence of a desire to photograph is relatively slight. For example, it is worth pointing out that the discursive desire to photograph often precedes the scientific knowledge needed to successfully do so. Virtually every account of the invention of photography begins with an 'impossible' idea, which is then slowly but surely brought to fruition in the face of constant scientific difficulties and uncertainties. Despite plenty of opportunities, there are no episodes in which this idea arose directly from scientific experiment and discovery itself. Similarly, the archive reveals that portraiture—so often said by historians to be photography's primary aspiration—is only occasionally and belatedly mentioned by its inventors as a possible future use for the medium. What such investigations might suggest in fact is that the evolutionary, percussive, cause and effect, base/superstructure notion of historical development that underlies many of these explanations is simply not appropriate to the empirical data we have on photography's emergence.

So how is one to read a desire to photograph against the timing of its emergence? We might well begin by noting the broader significance of this timing. For it soon becomes clear that the epistemological status of all the objects in which the proto-photographers want to invest their rhetorical desire—landscape, nature, the camera image—is at this same moment in the midst of an unprecedented crisis. What is particularly interesting about this crisis, this 'profound upheaval' as Foucault wants to call it, is that what appears to be at issue is not just the representation of Nature but, more fundamentally, the nature of representation itself.

> In a more fundamental fashion, and at the level where acquired knowledge is rooted in its positivity, the event concerns, not the objects aimed at, analysed, and explained in knowledge, not even the manner of knowing them or rationalizing them, but the relation of representation to that which is posited in it ... What came into being ... is a miniscule but absolutely essential displacement, which toppled the whole of Western thought ...[20]

Letters from an Exile at Botany-Bay, a small publication written in 1794 by Australia's first professional painter, Thomas Watling, can be used to exemplify the confusion accompanying the 'essential displacement' that Foucault describes.[21] Watling himself called his publication 'this heterogeneous and deranged performance' and warned his readership, 'not however expecting connection, you must just accept of each wild idea as it presents itself'. Watling consistently complains in his essay of the difficulty of representing, whether by word or image, the unfamiliar and untrustworthy characteristics of the new landscape to which he had been exiled. As a consequence, it is his surprise at, and uncertainty about, the veracity of his own observations that are the most striking sentiments to be found in his discourse. As Watling laments, 'never did I find language so imperfect as at present'.

In an elegant reading of Watling's publication, Ross Gibson points not only to the author's declared hesitations but also to the text's 'uneven' quality as 'an unruly and confused dissertation', and to its 'enunciative fitfulness'. Significantly, Gibson puts this fitfulness down, not to incompetence, but to 'the pressures that prevailed upon a creative subject attempting to "methodise" experience at the time of white Australia's inauguration'. As Gibson points out, the effects of this pressure are inscribed in the very rhetorical figurations adopted by Watling's prose.

> From start to finish a kind of alternating current runs through *Letters*, coursing back and forth between the one pole of expressionist subjectivity and the other of scientific objectivity, between the linguistic figures of metaphor and metonym ... His persona thus becomes traumatised; he becomes an effect of his own authorial dilemma.[22]

Gibson sees this authorial dilemma—a dilemma apparently involving a threat to the certainty of Watling's own subjectivity—as arising on the one hand from Watling's need to negotiate 'an aesthetic crisis that was also inherently theological' and on the other hand 'as a symptom of the upheaval that was occurring in the history of Western ideas at the end of the eighteenth century'. What makes this example so useful is that the crisis that Watling's text embodies is seen to encompass not only a questioning of representation and the objects posited in it, but also the West's prevailing orders of both knowledge (theological as well as empirical) and subjectivity.

And what of that latent desire that will in 1839 come to be called by the name photography? For contemporary historians informed by psychoanalysis, such a question 'pushes the invention of photography back beyond the nineteeth century', locating it instead within a conveniently universal narrative about the human subject's need to protect itself 'against the loss of the object (i.e. the always absent real object of desire), and the loss of identity'.[23] Desire, according to this model, is produced in the gap between need and demand. But this kind of account, with its continuing emphasis on the transhistorical constitution of the *individual* human subject, seems unable to account for the specificity of either the timing or the morphology of the generalised photographic desire described in this paper. Even if we accept that photography operates as yet another process of substitution for a lack, we are still left wondering why it should be this solution, and not some other, that arises around 1800, and not some other time, to fill what is supposed to be a perennial gap in our subjectivity. Psychoanalysis, in other words, seems unable to account for either cultural specificity or historical change.

This is no doubt why Foucault speaks of the profound changes he sees as taking place around 1800 ('something which is undeniable, once one has looked at the texts with sufficient attention'[24]), not as a matter of individual or even collective desire but as a '*positive unconscious* of knowledge'.[25]

> My problem was to ascertain the sets of transformations in the regime of discourses necessary and sufficient for people to use these words rather than those, a particular type of discourse rather than some other type, for people to be able to look at things from such and such an angle and not some other one.[26]

The fact that such transformations elude the consciousness of those involved in them suggests that discursive activity produces us, even as we produce discourse. Moreover Foucault goes on to make it clear in later books that any regimentation of what can and cannot be thought at a particular moment in history is as much a question of power as it is of knowledge. Indeed his concept of a 'positive unconscious' is soon replaced, via Nietszche, by the phrase 'will to power', and it is in these terms that he subsequently investigates the emergence of a variety of heterogeneous social apparatuses around the turn of the nineteenth century.

> I understand by the term 'apparatus' a sort of—shall we say—formation which has as its major function at a given historical moment that of responding to an *urgent need*. The apparatus thus has a dominant strategic function . . . The apparatus is thus always inscribed in a play of power, but it is always linked to certain coordinates of knowledge which issue from it but, to an equal degree, condition it. This is what the apparatus consists in: strategies of relations of forces supporting, and supported by, types of knowledge.[27]

During his investigations Foucault notices that a 'strange empirico-transcendental doublet . . . which was called *man*, . . . a being such that knowledge will be attained in him of what renders all knowledge possible', is produced as an integral, indeed necessary, component within each of these apparatuses.[28] This being is, he says, a completely new development, 'an invention of recent date . . . a figure not yet two centuries old'.[29] Foucault's discussion of the panopticon, that now notorious system of incarceration proposed by Jeremy Bentham in the late eighteenth century, is particularly interesting in this context. For this is an apparatus that, like photography and as the word's French appellation suggests (*appareil*: apparatus, camera), operates according to a certain system of relations between a light source, a focusing cell and a directed looking. According to Foucault, it is this same system of relations that extends into modern society as 'an indefinitely generalizable mechanism of "panopticism"'.[30]

It is worth noting that Foucault's emphasis on the workings of the panopticon has frequently been misread as a description of a 'static, spatial structure' designed to allow an oppressive surveillance of those without power by those who have it.[31] In fact Foucault is putting an argument that is far less simplistic than this. He reiterates Bentham's own point that as the 'prisoner' never knows when he is actually being watched, he must assume that it is always so; thus he necessarily surveys and disciplines himself. As far as the exercise of power is concerned, the prisoner is always caught in an uncertain space of hesitation between tower and cell. He is both the prisoner and the one who imprisons. 'He inscribes in himself the power relations in which he simultaneously plays both roles; he becomes the principle of his own subjection'.[32] The panopticon is, in other words, a productive exercise of subject formation operating such that its participants 'are not only its inert or consenting target; they are always also the elements of its articulation'.[33] Thus Foucault reads panopticism's reverberating economy of gazes as constituting each of its contributors as a self-reflexive doublet—as both the subject and object, effect and articulation of a net-like exercise of disciplinary power.

We might usefully read the apparatus of photography in similar terms. As it happens the desire to photograph is expressed by those pioneers gazing with frustration into their camera obscuras in circular and contradictory terms that are remarkably reminiscent of Foucault's account of panopticism. The first attempts to describe photo-desire are in fact fraught with problems of nomenclature and articulation, problems that are themselves suggestive of an unresolved philosophical uncertainty. What one finds, as in the three examples by Niépce, Daguerre and Talbot that follow, is an attempt at the level of language to maintain a reflexive movement that comes to rest at neither of the two possible poles that present themselves.

That's to say

1. Painting by nature herself
2. Copy by nature herself
3. Portrait by nature herself } Roughly
4. To show nature herself
5. Real nature
6. True copy from nature

Physaute } nature herself
Phusute

Autophuse
Autophyse } copy by nature[34]

In conclusion, the DAGUERREOTYPE is not merely an instrument which serves to draw Nature; on the contrary it is a chemical and physical process which gives her the power to reproduce herself.[35]

Some Account of the Art of Photogenic Drawing, or, The Process by Which Natural Objects May Be Made to Delineate Themselves without the Aid of the Artist's Pencil . . .[36]

We are given a sense here of the desire to photograph as something appearing on the cusp of two eras and two different world-views, something uncomfortably caught between, in Foucault's terms, the Classical and the Modern. The inference is that it is from this palpable sense of being neither completely one nor the other that the frustrations voiced by Watling, Gilpin, Coleridge and the proto-photographers all have their source. Some historians have tried to argue that photography was in fact a conceptual effort to reconcile these tensions, to resolve prevailing representational uncertainties and provide a positivist confirmation of an objective and discrete outside reality: 'The invention of photography may be seen as part of an effort, begun in the later eighteenth century, to remove the traces of an intervening, mediating consciousness from artistic production.'[37]

Strangely, this desire for a positivist certainty is again absent from the discourse produced by the proto-photographers (although it certainly appears as a dominant concern amongst commentators in mid-century and beyond). Consider again the concept-metaphor the proto-photographers conjure up to relieve their frustration—a mode of representation that is simultaneously fixed and transitory, that draws nature while allowing her to draw herself, that both reflects and constitutes its object, that partakes equally of the realms of nature and culture.[38] It would seem that the desire to photograph is here being projected—as its own nomenclature will later confirm (*photography*: light writing, light writing itself)—in terms of a will to power that is able to write itself even as it is written. Situated within a general epistemological crisis that has made the relationship between nature and her representations a momentarily uncertain one, photography is conceived in these first imaginings as something that is neither one nor the other, but is at the same time a parasitical spacing that encompasses and inhabits both.

The desire to photograph would therefore seem, at its inception at least, to involve a reproduction of that same empirico-transcendental economy of power-knowledge-subject which has made its own conception possible. This is a process of reproduction that doesn't operate only as ideology (the 'idea' of photography). Nor are its effects confined just to the finished photograph and those depicted in it. For the discourse of photo-desire confirms that we must, as Foucault puts it, 'grasp subjection in its material instance as a constitution of subjects' and this includes the photographer as much as the photographed.[39] Consider for a moment how the photographer, for whom the camera is, as Niépce put it, 'a kind of artificial eye', is constituted by photography as the prosthetic trope around and through which the complicitous economy of photo-desire necessarily turns.[40] This conjunction of photographer and camera produces more than just a surface reorganisation of power; it is productive of a total symbiotic assemblage such that 'power relations can materially penetrate the body in depth'.[41] To put this Foucauldian proposition simply, if photography is a mapping of bodies in time and space, then it is also a material production of those bodies, just as it is a reproduction of modernity's particular conception of the time/space continuum.

Photography as a latent *historical* force is reminiscent of the desire described with such relish by Deleuze and Guattari in *Anti-Oedipus* and *A Thousand Plateaus*. They speak of wanting to 'introduce production into desire, and conversely, desire into production'; their positive, rhyzomatic view of desire is thus analogous to Foucault's notion of power.[42]

> The truth of the matter is that *social production is purely and simply desiring production itself under determinate conditions*. We maintain that the social field is immediately invested by desire, that it is the historically determined product of desire, and that libido has no need of any mediation or sublimation, any psychic operation, any transformation, in order to invade and invest the productive forces and the relations of production. *There is only desire and the social, and nothing else*.[43]

> Desire has nothing to do with a natural or spontaneous determination; there is no desire but assembling, assembled, desire. The rationality, the efficiency, of an assemblage does not exist without the passions the assemblage brings into play, without the desires that constitute it as much as it constitutes them.[44]

There may be a danger in following too slavishly the historical path traced in this paper, a danger that one might end up having merely constructed a new beginning, a beginning seemingly more pure and essential, more true to photography's 'original identity', than that provided by the account it seeks to displace. However the greater danger is in assuming that the question of origins, a question one cannot escape even if one would want to, is ever anything *but* dangerous. By shifting the focus of the question from a singular moment of invention to the general appearance of a certain desiring production, photography's emergence is at least made an inescapably political issue. The writing of its history must henceforth address itself not just to developments in optics, chemistry and individual creativity, but to the production of a peculiarly modern inflection of power, knowledge and subject. This inflection inhabits in all its complexities the very grain of photography's existence as an event in our culture. Thus a beginning which was once thought to be fixed and dependable is now revealed as a problematic field of mutable historical differences. That is not a bad ending from which to begin again. To give Foucault the last word: 'What is found at the historical beginning of things is not the inviolable identity of their origin; it is the dissension of other things. It is disparity.'[45]

JENNIFER BIDDLE

3 Dot, circle, difference: *Translating Central Desert paintings*

This chapter is about the representation of Central Desert acrylic paintings. The growing number of desert art texts attest to the unprecedented success of these paintings in their progression from desert communities to galleries in Sydney, Paris and New York. As one recent Central Desert art text puts it, this

> rich and complex contemporary art form . . . is giving Aboriginal people a new sense of dignity and purpose, and is convincing white Australians and the world to perceive them and this continent with different eyes.[1]

That these paintings have been a success for their producers is not in question here. Rather, it is the terms in which this success is dependent upon a 'new' European eye, an eye which, as this chapter seeks to discern, may not be very different from its predecessor's. Issue is taken below with one of these art texts, *Kuruwarri: Yuendumu Doors.*[2] However, the criticisms raised here are in no way confined to this text, nor, it should be stressed, levelled at the authors/artists involved. The chapter seeks instead to identify a certain implicit politics in operation; a politics which may not simply be rectified by the current self-determining ethos which finds Aborigines to be authors of these—their own—representations. There can be no guarantee that involving community members, and their good intentions, in the production of such representations will result in different or less harmful images of 'Aboriginality'.[3]

Yuendumu Doors, according to the Australian Institute of Aboriginal Studies (AIAS) press release, is a 'remarkable book', a 'bilingual English/Aboriginal art book', a 'bilingual dreaming book'.[4] We, the readers, are invited to share in this event, to find not only 30 paintings produced by members of the Warlukulangu Artists' Collective on the school doors of Yuendumu, but their 'traditional dreaming stories', witnessed here first-hand since both Warlpiri transcripts and English translations accompany the paintings. Moreover, the text contains a description of the community, maps of both Yuendumu and the 'dreaming sites', even an 'Afterword' on the hermeneutics of Central Desert art—all attempts to supplement the difficult and elusive task of translating the 'meaning' of these paintings. A task which the text is not insensitive to, disclaiming as it does the possibility of 'full understanding' given the necessarily 'partial' comprehension the translations can contain.[5] In short, *Yuendumu Doors* should be remarkable, given its inclusions, its sensitivity and its authenticity. How then to explain my own disquiet, to make sense of my recalcitrance? Why do I remain unconvinced?

I could begin by pointing out the more pragmatic problem with the text's claim to bilingualism. For a start, the texts were not written independently in both English and Warlpiri by persons who can write in both languages. It is a translated text: a text of written Warlpiri vernacular and English translations of specifically oral Warlpiri stories. Further, bilingualism is a condition of subjects, not of texts. A text can only be bilingual in so far as it is *received* by subjects who are bilingual; a reception requiring in this case subjects who read both Warlpiri and English. Obviously, the number of non-Warlpiri subjects in this category are few, countable almost by name, for those Europeans who have proficiency in Warlpiri have made careers through their endeavours.

There are few Europeans who speak Aboriginal languages, but more perhaps who speak Warlpiri than any other, given the history of Warlpiri linguistic research and the (ongoing) Warlpiri Dictionary Project. This has meant, importantly, that very early on in the history of orthographising Aboriginal languages, Warlpiri had a standardised written form. The consequences for translation in this context are profound, given that the very development of written Warlpiri cannot be easily disentangled from an already (implicit) translation from and to English. Warlpiri was originally written by English speakers, borrowing its (modified) orthography, morphology and punctuation. The Warlpiri Dictionary is a Warlpiri to English dictionary, one designed for use by those assumed literate in English, and indeed the majority of Warlpiri writers and literacy workers are, almost by definition, literate in English, often having learnt English literacy first. The writing of Warlpiri has therefore, simutaneously, been its translation into English. Where, in this context, can (written) English be said to end and (written) Warlpiri begin?[6]

The text of *Yuendumu Doors* further excludes the greater number of Warlpiri subjects, for the text translates not bi-directionally but uni-directionally, from Warlpiri to English. The thoughtful discussions of the paintings, of the translations and of the landscape, are not translated into Warlpiri; they appear in English only.[7] One assumes they do not require translation, that this text is therefore intended for a 'non-Aboriginal' readership (as indeed, the press release states) and that it therefore cannot be bilingual. But, given that the English reader cannot read the Warlpiri, what purpose does its inclusion serve? Why present the Warlpiri transcript at all?

I do not pose this question lightly. The presentation of these 'dreaming' stories in Warlpiri, and thence in English, differentiates *Yuendumu Doors* from the growing number of Central Desert art texts.[8] These supplements authorise the Warlukurlangu artists in a dual sense, as authors of the paintings/stories and as authors of this text. It is the inclusion of these stories, the presence of Warlpiri voices, which places *Yuendumu Doors*, as the title of Eric Michael's Afterword suggests, within a 'postmodern' concern with representation, allowing the historical Other, the Aborigine, to speak for himself.[9] But it is this inclusion of Warlpiri voices, speaking here to the European reader only through translation, which may serve to exclude itself. Or rather, may serve to include something else. It is the presence of this something else, that is, of the absence of unmediated Warlpiri or Warlukurlangu voices, that this paper seeks to establish.

But first a proviso. I want to make clear what I am not arguing. I am not necessarily arguing that the Yuendumu artists have been misrepresented. To argue this would require an alternative, authoritative perspective, one necessarily denied me as I am not Warlpiri. I am positioned here instead as one who must rely on the translations as a guide; one who must therefore take issue not with misrepresentation or even representation but with presentation itself. And it is translation which is the dominant textual form that *Yuendumu Doors* presents.

The terms of translation I wish to address here are specific. Of course, the entire text represents a number of translation techniques: from spoken to written language; from painting to photograph; from implicit encodings to explicit decodings; culture to culture. At this stage I will ignore these more general senses of translation and confine my discussion to the role of the specifically linguistic: the supplementary stories the text provides. These stories are particularly salient as they accompany not only the *Yuendumu Doors* reproductions, but every reproduction of Central Desert art, every Central Desert canvas bought and sold.

Barthes' early analysis of one role the linguistic text performs in a relationship between image (visual) and text (linguistic) is useful here. He argues that when a linguistic message accompanies an image, it serves to 'anchor' or 'fix' a specific meaning from a range of imagic possibilities.[10] The stories, or their translations in this case, may serve less to provide additional information or to guide interpretation (as is their pretence) than to firmly 'anchor' one particular meaning from the paintings. This presentation of the painting as primary and the story as its accompaniment—a hierarchy in all Central Desert art texts—is itself problematic. Munn, who worked with the Warlpiri on these representations prior to their transfer onto canvas, argues that it is the story which is primary, the marking (previously on sand or body) the 'supplement to verbal expression'.[11]

A perfect translation is not, of course, possible. The 'sense of understanding one can obtain from a translation' as the text itself assents, is always 'spurious'.[12] But there is a great deal of movement, a great deal of semantic play between perhaps a 'better' translation and one less 'good'. If translation can never reproduce or replicate the original then the very sense of what distinguishes a 'good' from a less 'good' translation becomes itself a critical point. For while we may agree upon the impossibility of reproducing the original, we may disagree on what to do with this knowledge. How then to translate?

Translation is, as Walter Benjamin has argued, a 'mode'.[13] He invokes the term 'mode' to remind us that translation is no passive act; to warn us against assuming its secondary status as a translucent screen over what remains the primary, the original. Translation, Benjamin argues, announces the very 'death' of the original because it 'canonises' the original, freezing it forever into permanence; one cannot translate a translation, only an original. The original in many respects owes its existence, its 'life', to the translation. We only know the original from the 'life' or 'after-life' translation offers. It is the 'Task of the Translator', the title of Benjamin's thesis, to give life to the original. And in specific terms.

Benjamin begins with a number of complex negations, exemplifying what translation cannot be, or rather should not be, and his analysis must be read as much as an indictment of translation as it is a plea for its potentialities. His first argument is one against the idea of translation as a 'transmitting' device. To seek through translation a 'transmittable' essence is to seek what is, in fact, not obtainable in the original. He asks:

> For what does a literary work 'say'? What does it communicate? It 'tells' very little to those who understand it. Its essential quality is not statement or the imparting of information. Yet any translation which intends

> to perform a transmitting function cannot transmit anything but information—hence, something inessential. This is the hallmark of bad translation.[14]

Translation is not, for Benjamin, a matter of simply changing the exterior form, to reproduce in different words what remains an essential content. Translation cannot capture content, for the original is not content. The original does not stand in relation to an objective referent—information, quantifiable essence—but stands instead in a relation to language.

Translation then is not so much a problem of accounting for the original as it is a problem of the relationship between language and language, as Benjamin writes in an often-quoted passage: 'All translation is only a somewhat provisional way of coming to terms with the foreignness of languages.'[15]

Benjamin aligns translation with the task of philosophy, of literary theory and of history. Translation cannot 'render', 'copy' or 'reproduce': can philosophy 'paraphrase' the world, literary theory 'copy' a text, history 'imitate' the past? Though a specific mode, translation, as de Man claims, shares with these disciplines 'the fact that they do not resemble that from which they derive . . . they are all interlinguistic: they relate to what in the original belongs to language and not to meaning as an extralinguistic correlate.'[16]

Benjamin employs a striking image to illustrate this relation of translation to language. He speaks of a shattered vessel, the fragments of which need to 'match' each other in order to be reglued together. However, Benjamin stipulates that these fragments, though in detail must align, 'need not be like one another'.[17] That is, the relationship between original and translation is not one of resemblance and is not metaphoric but more synecdochic. He concludes:

> So instead of making itself similar to the meaning, to the Sinn of the original, the translation must, rather, lovingly and in detail, in its own language, form itself according to the manner of meaning of the original, to make both recognisable as the broken parts of a greater language, just as fragments are the broken part of a vessel.[18]

What Benjamin suggests here is important. If anything can be reproduced through translation it is the manner in which the original (fragment) is related to language (whole). However, it should be noted, as de Man does, that these language fragments can never reconstitute a complete whole.[19] Language is not entirely constituted in itself, still less in our knowledge of it. The figurative aspect of language serves to continually re-fragment and re-arrange the incompleted whole of meaning. The translative task for Benjamin is one of creation: of constructing a semantic province which can situate the translation within the second language as the original situates itself within its own language. And for Benjamin this requires a certain amount of literary licence.

Benjamin insists that the language of translation must 'let itself go . . . as its own kind of *intentio*'.[20] Translation is to 'open itself up' to the 'foreignness' of meaning, to the difference which the fragments and their arrangements can convey. In short, Benjamin argues for a translation of 'errancy': a roaming questful translative mode. He quotes Pannwitz on this point:

> Our translators, even the best ones, proceed from a wrong premise. They want to turn Hindi, Greek, English into German instead of turning German into Hindi, Greek, English. Our translators have a far greater reverence for the usage of their own language than for the spirit of foreign words . . . The basic error of the translator is that he preserves the state in which his own language happens to be instead of allowing his language to be powerfully affected by the foreign tongue.[21]

What does this have to do with *Yuendumu Doors*? First, it seems that the translations here suffer from being both not literal enough and from being entirely too literal. The fine line between 'fidelity and freedom', which Benjamin insists upon, is missed.

Purely in terms of form, the translations are not literal enough. They do not engage the reader with the 'foreignness' of language. Indeed, one is encouraged to 'read' the translations (separated physically as they are from the transcript by a page) without engaging with the Warlpiri at all. The text is laid out with the paintings reproduced (in colour) on the right-hand page, the Warlpiri (verbatim) story on the left page. Turning the page, one then finds the English translation on the right. Below it, a reduced skeletal reproduction of the painting is provided, where pointers link names (Warlpiri and English) to the black and white outline of the 'icons'. In order for the English reader to simultaneously read the story and look at the painting they must either flip back and forth between pages, or be content (as the layout encourages) with the 'iconographic' reproductions.

The metaphor here is one of separation—no dialogue allowed, a point I return to below. The transcriptive/translative mode offered by Muecke *et al*, following Tedlock, is preferable, for at least here the juxtaposition between the two languages is available.[22] But I would go further still, ironically in this case, and argue for an even more literal rendition: a word-by-word breaking down of the text to indicate the semantic difficulty which is Warlpiri.[23] The text claims that a 'direct word for word translation would be very difficult for the English speaker to follow'[24]; but why should it be easy? Why should cultural confrontation, the breaking with one's codes, not be disruptive? Is coming to terms with foreignness, with difference, ever easy?

On the other hand, the 'content' of the translations are too literal, in Benjamin's sense. These are translations which intend to 'transmit'. As the AIAS press release states: 'It is hoped that this unique book, *Yuendumu Doors*, will give non-Aborigines some sense of the understanding of these traditional dreamtime paintings and stories . . .[25]

Since these stories are presumably 'about' the paintings, this content is translated literally. The iconographic 'keys' which accompany the transcripts (and indeed accompany all reproductions of Central Desert paintings) cements this transmitting mode: here is a *karnta* (woman); this a *wardapi* (goanna). Here the translation does far worse than that which Benjamin warns against—transmitting essence—it points, metonymically, at that to which it refers.[26] The maps here perform a similar function, iconographically deferring to essential phenomena which it seems are merely then copied by the paintings, reproduced in the Warlpiri voice and translated—pure facsimile—into English.

What worries me here is not necessarily what the paintings or the stories 'really' mean but rather what the translative mode says they mean. What worries me is precisely what Benjamin tends to pass over in his account of translation—the determinative effects of the translative posture. In this case it is the overburdening, the omnipresence of the ultimate referent, archetypally that of 'landscape'. What worries me is how this translative mode serves to reinforce an already over-determined portraiture, a portraiture which speaks at once of the Aborigine as Other and therefore of the difference which is Us. These productive effects of translation are what I now seek to establish.

I do not query that these paintings/stories are about the 'land' (or in this case, 'dreaming sites and paths', flora and fauna, bush edibles and 'dreamtime beings'. All are found as synonyms for, and with, 'land' in the text.) I query that they are only about the 'land' and in the manner the text depicts. The aligning of the paintings with the cartographic maps of Yuendumu, of the school, and of the 'dreaming sites' (where 'North is approximately to the left'[27]) is unfortunate. It actively encourages a 'decoding' interpretation, one in which deciphering the relationship between icon and referent, symbol and landscape becomes the primary task. The dominance of this deciphering of the 'icons' is marked in this and other Central Desert art texts (cf. note 8). It is as if the European reader almost delights in (finally?) being able to understand something the Aborigine is saying. This perhaps explains, too, something of the success of the paintings, perhaps equally on behalf of the artists who take active part in the production of this understanding, complicit in providing the European with some tangible 'key', as it were.

A slightly different reading might see these paintings as a form of recently developed communication in these terms, one operating directly between the Desert artist and the European reader. This communicative form is specifically unlike that of pigeon, creole or Aboriginal English—there is no sense in which this communication is not Aboriginal; no sense in which the European can speak back. That the European cannot fully understand these 'icons', the paintings, something again which all the texts go to some length to assure us of, satisfies both ends of the exchange: on the one hand, increasing the authority of the Central Desert artist's rights of knowledge, of propriety, and, on the other hand, further exoticising and mystifying the painting (the 'landscape', the Aborigine) for the European.

However, reading of *Yuendumu Doors* is reduced to rendition, precisely an 'exercise in cartographics', despite the Afterword's warning. This mapping metaphor, the apparent reducible iconicity of the paintings, suggests that, not unlike the stories translated, the paintings' meanings are purely a matter of differing form. It suggests they are obscure but simple signifiers (hence learnable by following the keys) of what remains the only possible referent, the determinative signified, the land. Here the paintings become not complex semiotics of a landscape constructed, but primitive imitations of it.

This distinction between primitive symbolism and creative signification derives from a history of the philosophy of language which has privileged the spoken word over that of the written, and subsequently, that of the Western speaker/reader over that of any other writer/reader.[28] The Peircian linguistic hierarchy[29] most resembles the framework implicitly deployed in the treatment of Central Desert 'art'. For Peirce, the icon is relegated to that of first-order symbolism. It is said to bear a resemblance to, or exhibit the same qualities as, the object it denotes. The sophisticated graduant, the sign proper, the word, is said to bear none. The conceptual relegation of these paintings to that 'iconicity', beginning with the work of Munn[30] and subsequently reproduced in all Central Desert art texts, including *Yuendumu Doors*, is deemed to operate in the first and more innocent instance to exclude. No indication is given that these paintings are also about history; self and identity; social relations; the rights to tell/paint these stories and indeed that they are establishing moments of these rights.[31] In short, no indication is proffered that these paintings are properly 'semiotic'—productive and effectual of a density of meanings. Why do these meanings not translate? Why the iconic prevalence?

A partial answer to this question may be reached by a short detour through the circumstances of the production of these paintings.

Unlike in northern Australia, where images figured historically upon more permanent materials (bark or wood), Central Desert images were drawn in the sand or on the body. It wasn't until 1971 at Papunya that an art teacher, Geoff Bardon, in inviting some men to paint the school walls, was instrumental in these designs being rendered transferable to canvas. The creation of the acrylic painting as object of attention, comment and permanence has shifted the focus of interpretion from that of the productive aspects of these paintings to that of interpreting their status as product. This is a problematic status for images historically marked by their capacity for erasure—images that are produced within performative or enactive contexts where the production of the designs (who is allowed to mark whom with what and when) is inseparable from the ensuing product itself.

Resituating these paintings/stories from aesthetic considerations to a broader historical and political context, it can be seen that Central Desert 'paintings' are a very recent phenomemon. They emerged historically just prior to the Northern Territory Land Rights Act of 1976, the subsequent outstation movement which saw Aborigines return to their lands and the concomitant growth in Aboriginal self-determination and self-management politics. Their emergence must be read (as von Sturmer notes in relation to the 'sudden flowering' of Aboriginal oral histories[32]) against this background in which Aboriginal accounts, including paintings, begin to provide the fuel to counter, augment and rewrite the Eurocentric version of Australia's occupation. To the extent that the stories in *Yuendumu Doors* speak of the 'land', they do so in a climate where establishing rights over the land has been the *sine qua non* of the Aborigine/European encounter, and the extent to which these stories and paintings may serve to contribute to the Aboriginal record is worthy of praise. But the extent to which this climate is taken for granted by the text is problematic.

Yuendumu Doors presents its 'traditional dreaming stories' as if they were flat anthropological facts: *the* stories. Not only does this serve to mask the fact that these stories may be told differently on any number of occasions,[33] thus preserving the hackneyed assumption that Aboriginal stories, like their religion and their relations to the land, are static and timeless. It also masks the fact that, in this case, these stories were told *to someone*. These stories are not *the* one and only dreaming story but a story told at a particular moment to a particular auditor. The stories, if not the paintings, were elicited with the express purpose of recording them for a European audience—a context no less authentic and perhaps no less traditional now that the Central Desert artists have for some time been asked by Europeans to 'tell the story'.[34] But this context, and its effects, is nevertheless not avowed in the text.

Michel Foucault has criticised the naive assumption of a passive listening subject. In relation to the nineteenth century confessional, he reverses the assumption that the elicitor merely serves to invite a response from the teller, allowing her/his authoritative words to reign, and argues instead that

> the agency of domination does not reside in the one who speaks (for it is he who is constrained), but in the one who listens and says nothing; not in the one who knows and answers, but the one who questions and is not supposed to know.[35]

What this suggests is that the 'role of listening' is largely productive, if not determinative of, the stories. *Yuendumu Doors* stories abound with claims of veracity, of ownership of land, and of what might be crudely called 'cultural resilience', that is, the continuing right to make these claims to truth and to ownership. I am not suggesting that claims to truth and propriety were not part of traditional story telling. I note the extent to which these features are now marked. On veracity, for instance, Paddy Japaljarri Stewart speaks of '... relating these true stories of the Dreamtime' and, later, extends this truth claim to his entire Honey Ant 'story':

> This Honey Ant Dreaming is a true story. This Dreaming is right here where we are living, on this land at Yuendumu. I am telling this true Dreamtime story just as our ancestors told us. It is because of them that we are telling about these Dreaming tracks. We are telling this story exactly as we can. We are not making it up. It really is true![36]

On the ownership of land, Larry Jungarrayi Spencer 'told':

> The land of this story and painting belongs to us. It is our own. Our fathers left it to us a long time ago.[37]

On the continuity between this truth and proprietary rights, Paddy Japaljarri Simms 'told':

> They (the fathers in the Dreamtime) used (witi poles) when they initiated young men, as we do today ... They instructed us in the Warlpiri law and told us not to forget what we had been taught; told us to hold on our law and follow it the right way.[30]

Or, the version Paddy Japaljarri Stewart gave of this:

> We follow the Dreaming and speak truthfully about it ... We follow many important Dreamings. Our grandfathers told us the story of the Dreaming and now we are relating it.[39]

These selections are indiction. They are 'stories' which speak to the uninformed, the unknowing, the uninitiated. They are attempting to instruct, consciously delineating a 'we who know' from an audience that does not. They seek recognition—to persuade, convince, establish. They speak to an audience lacking persuasion or conviction. They bear witness to an omitted addressee, a European 'listener' who historically has failed to 'hear'. *Yuendumu Doors* does not suffer from this failure but perhaps from the converse: an over-attentive 'listening' which ignores its determinative receptive position.

The translations remain unsigned, unauthored throughout the text. The only indication of who these translators may be (with the exception of the first signed Warlpiri text and English translation by Tess Napaljarri Ross and Nickie Piper) is given euphemistically on the back cover as 'others in the community'. It is as if by denying this context, this 'listening role' augmented in translation, the terms of trade could simply be reversed. That is, as if by translating the monophonic 'authentic' Warlpiri voice (problematic at a most basic level, given that some of the paintings were jointly produced) the incongruent relations of power existing between the subjects communicating could cease. It is as if the translator could be nothing but an 'informed scribe',[40] and as if the Warlpiri 'voice' unmediated could alone speak. This condition, however, is simply not possible.

If, in effect, these 'stories' are instances in which Warlpiri artists address an uninformed audience (a specific or general European audience), one wonders why the text cannot represent this encounter. An inclusion of this 'listener', an opening up of the text to its own mediations, may not result in a more 'authentic' Warlpiri story, but it may result in a more 'authentic' realisation of the conditions in which the stories were produced. Forcing the European voice might force what is, in fact, already a confrontation; it might allow for the possible negation of what remains in the text a passive but productive role—the background silence against which the stories necessarily speak. It may also force the reader from his or her perceived role of passivity: a subject who hears without listening, who can 'read without interruption'[41] or acknowledgement and whose discrete and privileged identity is the *raison d'être* of the text provided.

I began this paper by arguing that a Warlukulangu or Warlpiri voice is absented from *Yuendumu Doors*. By this I mean absented in both senses described above: first, the overaligning of the paintings with an iconicity serves to exclude other meanings; and secondly, that this exclusion is as indicative of the listening audience as it is of the speaking subject. But there is a third unfortunate translative tendency operating here, one related to the above and dependent on the same conditions. I refer to the tendency for these stories (and I might add, for the majority of Aboriginal translations) to read with a childlike quality and, paradoxically, to fail to engage anyone but the academic reader in an appreciation of their richness. That is, even apparently 'good' Aboriginal translations, such as these, may require knowledge derived from outside the specific text at hand (a familiarity with Aborigines and their mode of story telling, for example).[42] The translations themselves do not bring this sense into the language of the translation.

One of the express purposes of *Yuendumu Doors* is to provide the reader with some sense of the 'complexities of Warlpiri religion and society', if only as an 'imperfect glimpse'. What the reader may discern, however, is the converse, greeted as they are by stories comprised of simple declarative sentences, copular verb forms and non-complex clauses, iconic keys and maps, and with content which informs of the Warlpiri ability to 'speak' only of the land, of the 'Dreamtime' and of mythic ancestors. In short, rather than enriching, *Yuendumu Doors* seems to perpetuate the portrayal of the Aborigine as suspended in an archaic era: noble but simple.

In this case the portrayal is valorised. Positive attributes are given to the same set of oppositions which first gave rise to the distinction between the savage and the civilised, the oral and the literate, the mythic and the historic, the simple and the complex: 'Them' and 'Us'. Perhaps even employing the term 'and' here between these terms is too mild, for the categories evoked are not so much contingent as they are exclusive. Like the economy of either/or witnessed above, where it seems historically either 'We' speak to 'Them' or just recently, 'They' to 'Us' (Warlpiri to European), this 'economy of difference' as Derrida might have it, posits no remainder.[43] The celebratory sentiment, the almost Thoreauian valorisation of the land unfortunately gets extended to the Warlpiri, the Aborigine himself, iconographically treated here as both an extension, and substitution for, 'land'.[44] This buoying-up of the second set of terms, which the opposition served initially to negate, by no means refuses the terms of the dichotomies, but proceeds within an economy which is ultimately of the same. Irrespective of the values involved in this type of redress, the text fails to revoke what historically has been perceived as that of the Aborigines' deficiency. As von Sturmer pointedly asks: 'Do images exist which can subvert the function they are expected to provide?'[45] The 'Doors' in this sense remain closed.

The 'economy of difference' I speak of here is not confined to the realm of metaphysics or metaphor. A very material, international economy persists in which these paintings are marketed. As Michaels puts it, these paintings 'strike a chord with issues and images being negotiated in art galleries of Sydney, Paris and New York'.[46] It may indeed be the case that it is the abstract modernism of the paintings which strikes the resounding chord, but it is also necessarily the image of the land-looking ethnographic Other which resounds: the stories always accompany the paintings. Within this economy, the stories provide a signature to the paintings, not in an individualistic sense, nor in the sense of artistic *oeuvre* as Michaels carefully points out[47] but collectively. These surprisingly similar sounding stories demarcate these paintings as specifically exotic, and serve primarily as signatures of the differentiation of the iconic from the semiotic and of primitive paintings from modern.[48] In short, the supplements in this case reveal an initial lack, the Aborigine/Other as not the European/Us.

Derrida argues that 'supplements' or 'additions' are never merely added on to given plenitudes but serve to fulfil initial absences or lacks, are revelatory of initial (hence remaining) absences. He argues further that the signature provides to the written text a sense of presence, of intention, of autonomy, of what remains the very absence of the author or of his/her control over the text and its effects.[49] The supplementary stories in the Central Desert case provide a signature to the paintings (the paintings are not 'signed' as in Western painting traditions), revealing not only the absences Derrida describes, nor the lack of an authentic Warlpiri voice as outlined above, but are revealing of a larger lack in which the Aborigine as Other is located.

Andrew Pekarik, owner of a Park Avenue art gallery in New York and jointly responsible for one of the largest published texts on Aboriginal Art,[50] visited Yuendumu and was quoted as saying that his intention in exhibiting these paintings was to illustrate 'that these people with practically zero material culture have one of the most complex and intellectual cultures of any society.'[51] Pekarik's stated aim, like that of *Yuendumu Doors*, is an optimistic one in the face of the economy, discussed above, operating in translation. Worse, or ironically better, what I call 'unfortunate translative tendencies' may be fortunate: the paintings sell perhaps because of, not despite, their stories. In this sense *Yuendumu Doors* is a success and the 'Doors' open. But only within terms which serve to exclude the Aboriginal voice, except when it speaks within the range of 'our' hearing.*

* An earlier version of this paper was presented in the Department of Anthropology, University of Sydney in November 1987. Since then, a number of people have contributed their comments. I would like to thank John von Sturmer, Alan Rumsey, Eric Michaels, Ian Bedford, Ann Game, Dennis Tedlock, Jennifer Rutherford, Anne Rutherford, Gertrude Stotz, Lee Cataldi, Robyn Ferrell and especially Ros Diprose. Any remaining deficiencies are mine. I spoke less Warlpiri at the time this paper was conceived than I do now. I would like to thank the Australian Institute of Aboriginal Studies and the Carlyle Greenwell Bequest provided by the Department of Anthropology, University of Sydney for making it possible to learn Warlpiri.

PART II
Of Bodies 1

PAUL PATTON

4 Nietzsche and the body of the philosopher

Nietzsche is commonly thought of as a philosopher who speaks in a loud voice. For Alexander Nehamas, the fact that Nietzsche 'shouts' is 'the most consistent and the most conspicuous feature of his writing'.[1] Descriptions of his writing as 'strident' or 'bombastic' are common, and there is no doubt that some passages, such as the early declamatory discourses of Zarathustra, are delivered in such tones. But this is not the only manner in which Zarathustra speaks, and there are passages elsewhere in his writing in which Nietzsche explicitly denigrates such modes of address.

In *The Gay Science*, for example, he asserts that 'anyone with a very loud voice is almost incapable of thinking subtleties'.[2] In fact, Zarathustra's initial attempts to speak to others fail disastrously. His subsequent more subtle thoughts are invariably proffered in a quieter voice: one thinks of the silent Zarathustra at the end of his convalescence, conversing with his soul in an inner voice 'of great longing'. What he longs for most of all is that this soul to whom he has given everything should assume a different voice, that it should *sing*. In doing so, it would become not only a voice of wisdom but the voice of an artist, a philosopher-artist or an aesthetic Socrates.

The combination of the loud voice and the stillest words within Nietzsche's texts presents a problem for readers, as indeed does the mixture of coarse and subtle ideas throughout his writing. Nehamas argues that the strident voice and the hyperbolic character of much of Nietzsche's writing is a device to attract the reader's attention. Alternatively, it might be seen to serve a masking function, the coarse external appearance of his extravagant prose hiding the delicate and profound thought which is only occasionally revealed therein. After all, Nietzsche tells us, 'every profound spirit needs a mask'.[3]

However, it is one thing to explain the combination of tones and voices in Nietzsche's writing, it is another to explain the overriding importance he attaches to the voice, to the tone and manner of speaking. In *Ecce Homo*, Nietzsche insists that it is not a prophet who speaks in *Zarathustra* and that 'above all, one must *hear* aright the tone that comes from this mouth, the halcyon tone, lest one should do wretched injustice to the meaning of its wisdom'.[4] It is this specifically philosophical voice which interests me here. What is the connection between the stillness of this 'voice' and the meaning of Nietzsche's innermost philosophy? What is the connection between this 'voice' and understanding the philosopher to be a certain kind of body, one which must be defined in terms of its characteristic powers, its preferred terrain or habitat?

BODIES AND POWERS

The justification for approaching Nietzsche's conception of the philosopher in this way lies in the zoological character of much of his own discourse. He rejects the traditional philosophical disdain for the body and insists upon the importance of the corporeal aspects of existence. He draws attention to such things as the particular bodily comportment of those used to exercising power, and speaks in terms of the proximate senses of smell and taste as well as the mediate ones of sight and hearing. He asserts that such things as nutrition, climate, place of residence and mode of recreation, in short 'the whole casuistry of selfishness', are 'inconceivably more important than everything one has taken to be important so far'.[5] More generally, Nietzsche constantly depicts human being as a special case of animal nature. Humankind is at once the sickliest and the most interesting of animals, the only one whose moral constitution has itself a history and thus the only one open to future possibilities. His attempts to categorise different types of human being rely heavily upon figures of animality: the beautiful cat 'woman' in *Beyond Good and Evil;* the mole critic of morality in the preface to *Daybreak*; the camel and lion at the outset of *Zarathustra*, as well as Zarathustra's own animals, the eagle and the serpent: respectively the proudest and the wisest animal under the sun. Nietzsche's project of distinguishing a new type or species of philosopher, a 'philosopher of the future', is also sometimes couched in these terms. The philosopher is a species of thinking animal and as such shares certain general characteristics with other animals:

> Every animal—therefore *la bête philosophe*, too—instinctively strives for an optimum of favorable conditions under which it can expend all its strength and achieve its maximal feeling of power . . .[6]

Ordinarily, different species of animal are identified by their bodies: a human has only two legs while a horse has four, and so on. However, this kind of observable morphological difference will not enable us to distinguish among bipeds *les bêtes philosophes*, for these come in all shapes and sizes as well as in different sexes. In order to specify the nature of the philosophical animal, we need a more general answer to the question: 'What is a body?' The commonsense biological view is that a body is a relatively autonomous thing, separated off from other bits of the world by an epidermal surface and endowed with its own distinctive mechanisms for motion, intake and digestion of raw materials, excretion and the like. In other words, a body must be autonomous in certain respects, but the question is in which? There are whole species whose reproduction depends upon specific interaction with other species. It seems then that what counts as an autonomous entity depends upon the perspective in which the question is asked. This is not only true in regard to biological bodies but more importantly, since the philosophical animal is not reducible to a biological or physiological kind, it is true of other sorts of bodies as well. Consider the classical conceptions of the body politic: what are the basic components of political society? Are they adult male individuals or are they adult male heads of households?

The question of autonomy aside, it may be argued that a body cannot be conceived independently of the kinds of relation it has with the world external to it. On this approach, a body may be considered as a more or less complex mechanism which selects and attaches to itself those things which enable it to grow, while selecting as well in order to avoid those things which threaten its integrity. However, such mechanisms of selection will be the effect of the specific combination of powers and capacities that make up the body. This approach therefore leads to a more general conception of bodies, one which defines them as complex assemblages of powers.

Insofar as we take this to be a concept of bodies as such, then it is an abstract conception. There is no overriding obligation to distinguish between animate and inanimate machines, no fundamental difference between bodies capable of thought and those only capable of executing a programme. The character of the forces which may constitute a body remains undetermined. These may be physical, moral, cultural or even aural forces:

> A body can be anything; it can be an animal, a body of sounds, a mind or an idea; it can be a linguistic corpus, a social body, a collectivity.[7]

Different kinds of bodies may be distinguished by the qualitative differences between capacities to affect and be affected by other bodies. On this approach, bodies will differ in kind as their capacities differ, and as the level of intensity of those capacities varies. So, for example, a feral cat may have more in common with a fox than with a domestic cat.

The notion of specific kinds of power is inseparable from a notion of bodies and vice versa. In each particular case, where we are dealing with specific powers, it is a matter of the nature or constitution of the body concerned and of the relationships into which it can enter with other bodies. For this reason, Deleuze and Guattari suggest:

> We know nothing about a body until we know what it can do, in other words, what its affects are, how they can or cannot enter into composition with other affects, with the affects of another body, either to destroy that body or be destroyed by it, either to exchange actions and passions with it or to join with it in composing a more powerful body.[8]

To describe bodies in this manner is to describe them in terms of their *power* in the primary sense of that term; that is, their capacity to act in certain ways or to enter into certain relations with other bodies; their capacity to do, to be or to become certain things, such as docile or invisible. Power in this sense has no necessary connection with what is usually thought of as political power, namely power *over* other bodies. It is a more abstract conception of power which covers the whole range of actions of bodies upon each other and upon themselves: actions which restrict or otherwise dominate the actions of others are only a subset of these. To conceive of bodies in this way, however, is to think of them as always embedded in networks of power relations, that is relations with other bodies. In describing the human body as object or point of application of disciplinary techniques, Foucault shows how a variety of early modern social theorists conceived of the body in this manner; that is, as a body composed of forces which it is the aim of discipline to enhance as well as to subject or dominate.[9]

Nietzsche also understands bodies in this manner, as composed of a multiplicity of forces which conspire together for their mutual benefit: 'my idea is that every specific body strives to become master over all space and to extend its force ... But it continually encounters similar efforts on the part of other bodies and ends by coming to an arrangement ('union') with those of them that are sufficiently related to it: thus they conspire together for power ...'[10] Power is thus the element out of which and within which bodies are constituted. Moreover, it is a dynamic element, one whose particular forms are governed by an inner will, instinct or desire which Nietzsche calls 'will to power'. This inner will is precisely the will to increase, to enhance itself in order to attain the maximal feeling of power. But what form this self-enhancement takes will depend upon the character of the body concerned.

In its most primitive forms, increase takes the form of incorporation of one body by another. This is a primitive mode of increase in the sense that, as more is ingested, the character of the body remains the same, only its dimensions vary. Although primitive, incorporation remains a significant model of power even for higher forms of animal or corporate life. Freud uses this model in his account of the oral stage of the human subject's development. The first drive of the neonate is that of incorporation. Similarly, his account in *Totem and Taboo* of the murder of the father makes reference to the act of devouring. Elias Canetti also makes incorporation in the most literal sense the central process of power.[11] Nietzsche sometimes gives the impression that this is the only form in which will to power manifests itself. The following passage is a typical remark: 'Life itself is *essentially* appropriation, injury, overpowering of the strange and weaker, suppression, severity, imposition of one's own forms, incorporation and, at the least and mildest, exploitation . . .'.[12]

It is clear, however, that the exploitation, appropriation and subjugation of weaker bodies by stronger can take many forms other than simple incorporation. Think of the history of forms of capture and appropriation of human labour power, from slavery through the forms of feudal and sovereign subordination to the modern system of exploitation of 'free' wage labour. Or think of the history of social relations between men and women.[13] A more general and flexible concept for this exploitative modality of the will to power may be found in the notion of *capture* which Deleuze and Guattari use to define the abstract form of the State. In general terms, capture involves the incorporation of other bodies, their powers and capacities. But capture only exists in its concrete manifestations, which include the whole panoply of mechanisms for the extraction or fixation of the forces of others: the patriarchal family, Bentham's panopticon or the conception of philosophy as a master-discourse of legitimation and foundation, are all apparatuses of capture.

Nevertheless, relations between bodies are by no means confined to the varieties of incorporation, subordination and domination. Nietzsche's conception of bodies as the result of 'union' between different forces already implies that other kinds of relation are also possible: relations of composition, for example, which occur whenever individual bodies enter into some form of common existence, thereby constituting new capacities or shifting those already present to a higher level of intensity. The formation of a political community or body politic may involve such enabling relations between disparate forces. In this case, the relations between forces or bodies that enter into such 'union' create the conditions for a transformation or metamorphosis which leads to the creation of a new body or a new kind of body. Historically, of course, such relations of mutual respect and enhancement have been instituted primarily between adult male heads of households, who continue to benefit from the captured forces of women. Nevertheless, these relations are not the same as those involved in capture—a qualitatively different kind of arrangement of powers is present. For this reason, Deleuze and Guattari contrast to the State-form another modality of the will to power, one which is embodied only in forms of non-sedentary life and which gives rise to the creative powers of movement and transmutation.

Power in this mode involves more than simply increase in the dimensions or capacities of a given body, it involves metamorphosis, transformation or becoming-other. Not simply the repetition of the same on a larger scale but the production of something different. The overall power of a body of this kind may thus be considered as a virtual sum of all its possibilities for transformation and modification. When Deleuze and Guattari speak of the becoming-horse of Freud's little Hans, or of the becoming-imperceptible of a writer such as F. Scott Fitzgerald, what they have in mind are capacities or affects of these particular bodies. These *affects* in turn are nothing more or less than the processes of transformation, the different metamorphoses or 'becomings' of which the body is capable.

Nietszche, too, constantly speaks of different species of human in terms of animal affinities: the 'wasted dogs' and cattle of the human herd on the one hand, Zarathustra's eagle and serpent on the other. The former stand for moral virtues, since the herd is a reactive formation, incapable of becoming anything other than what it is. The latter by contrast serve to name the actual or potential powers of the human animal, such as the pride entailed by Zarathustra's becoming-eagle. Whether in fact or in principle such powers are only realised in the exceptions, in the 'well-turned out' individuals, is another question. The central purpose of Nietzsche's philosophy is to evaluate existing values by reference to the ideal maximum, to 'the highest power and splendor actually possible to the type man'.[14]

From a practical point of view, the important thing is to know what kind of animal one is or is capable of becoming. For it is only on this basis that one can apply the ethical principles which flow from this way of understanding bodies and so determine the conduct of the appropriate kind of life. For example, one should avoid those other bodies and affects which tend to weaken or diminish one's power, while encouraging instead encounters and relations with other bodies which tend to enhance one's power. So far as individual bodies are concerned, Nietzsche's view is that the maximal feeling of power is attained only when the point is reached at which all action is an expression of the body's strength: 'A living thing seeks above all to *discharge* its strength.'[15] For some reactive, uncreative kinds of body this maximum will only be attained by virtue of dominance over others, but the most powerful bodies are those endowed with 'the bestowing virtue'. In general terms, the maximal feeling of power is attained when a body acts in perfect autonomy within the limits of its type. When this occurs, the body in question has reached a level of fullness or power such that anything further can only be a downfall or downgoing of the kind which Zarathustra praises in others and eventually undertakes himself: 'I love those who do not know how to live except their lives be a down-going . . .'[16]; 'I love him who wants to create beyond himself, and thus perishes.'[17]

Life of whatever kind is best served by the self-destructive action of such powerful bodies, those whose action can only enrich the physical or moral, communal or intellectual life in which they are engaged. As these examples suggest, however, such expenditure of power can never be merely undirected or uncontrolled explosions of force. For the point is to expend the type of force appropriate to the kind of animal one is: every animal strives for an optimum of favorable conditions under which it can expend *its* strength. So, what are the strengths of the philosophical animal?

PHILOSOPHERS OF THE FUTURE

Philosophers, as Nietzsche understands them, are creators of new values. They are producers of new interpretations since values are ultimately, for Nietzsche, interpretations of existence. This is their primary affect: the power of cultural or spiritual invention. But there is more than one kind of philosopher. The power to create new values may be realised in more than one mode. In the past, philosophers produced interpretations which sought to determine the nature and value of existence as a whole. Every great philosophy, Nietzsche suggests in an early essay, 'says only: this is the picture of all life, and learn from it the meaning of your own life.'[18]

To the extent that such interpretations seek to lay down once and for all the foundations of moral and natural law, they amount to forms of theoretical capture, constituting the equivalent in thought to the domains of interiority imposed by forms of State. 'Actual philosophers', Nietzsche suggests, 'are commanders and law-givers: they say "thus it shall be!" . . .'[19] Such philosophers may be characterised by a rule of sameness and a will to universalise. They exert power over others by means of their values and their doctrines of good and evil.

Whereas in the past the philosophical frame of mind had always been linked to the attainment of a single viewpoint upon life and events in general, Nietzsche suggests in *Human, All Too Human*, a different path to the enrichment of knowledge: rather than attempting to make themselves uniform, philosophers should listen 'to the soft voice of different life-situations'.[20] This insistence upon the value of plurality is one of Nietzsche's enduring commitments. Accordingly, the philosophers of the future will shun any pretension to universality: 'It must offend their pride, and also their taste, if their truth is supposed to be a truth for everyman. . .'.[21] Even Zarathustra teaches only *his* way, since *the* way does not exist.[22] As such, this is a paradoxical teaching. In the absence of any attempt to universalise, or to ensure the repetition of the same fundamental truths he has given them, what can be said about his disciples or followers? Only that they too will be, like him, creators of values. On his own account, Zarathustra is no more than 'a prologue to better players'.[23] More is said, however, by means of the forms of corporeality which Nietzsche attributes to the new philosophers. These are not metaphors, but ways of designating the powers and capacities of a new type of body, a new kind of philosophical animal.

At the end of the book, Zarathustra, the would-be creator, awaits his children. In other words, the philosopher's body as Nietzsche understands it is one which begets or bears; it is a *maternal* body, heavy with future thoughts, pregnant with new values. Just as the love of artists for their work may be regarded as a kind of maternal love, so may that of the philosophers for their creations. Along with this go a whole series of related affects, such as patience or timidity in the face of external forces, and a willingness to submit to whatever will not harm the product.[24] The character of these philosophical mothers may also involve a degree of selfishness, which only appears to contradict the affects mentioned above, since any theft to which it gives rise is always to the benefit of the child or the work rather than the bearer. Moreover, it is a selfishness which reinforces the Nietzschean philosopher's rejection of universality in favour of the particular, differential virtue: 'one is pregnant only with one's own child', Zarathustra tells the Higher Men.[25] These remarks provide one set of clues to Nietzsche's well known description of himself in *Ecce Homo* as 'the first psychologist of the eternally feminine'.[26]

We may wonder, however, whether such remarks are anything more than the revival of a familiar philosopheme which we find already in Plato's *Symposium*. Do they mean anything more than the appropriation of the specifically female power of gestation on behalf of the 'higher' creative desire of the soul? While Nietzsche's use of the language of pregnancy cannot be entirely divorced from this tradition, neither can it be confined to its prior forms. For the use of this language in relation to the philosophers of the future has effects upon both the concept of pregnancy and that of the philosopher. In the first place, as Alison Ainley points out, it is an active conception of the creative power, one which does not allow pregnancy to be conceived as the mere gestation of a seed imposed from without.[27] Second, the nature of childbirth serves to clarify the kind of creation expected of these philosophers of the future. A maternal body is one whose specific power is to give birth to something other than itself. It is therefore a body which does not simply repeat itself but rather becomes itself only by becoming-other. For this reason perhaps, Derrida describes Nietzsche as 'the thinker of pregnancy which, for him, is no less praiseworthy in a man than it is in a woman'.[28] If we can speak of repetition here, it is a repetition inseparable from the production of difference. The tension at the heart of Zarathustra's relation to his disciples may also be understood in these terms: they can only become his disciples by becoming something other than he.

At the end of the book, however, it is not disciples whom Zarathustra awaits but his children. This points to another important feature of the philosophers of the future: the fact that their creativity, if it is genuine, must be embodied. In *Daybreak*, Nietzsche comments that many of those 'in the great cities of world politics' who aspire to make a contribution nevertheless lack 'genuine productivity': 'However much they may desire to do great work, the profound speechlessness of pregnancy never comes to them!'.[29] In other words, giving birth to new values is essentially a corporeal event, not merely a speech act. In the case of Zarathustra himself, his transformation into one capable of expecting children is inscribed on his body, which has become light, like that of a dancer. But it is above all in qualities of the voice that his transformed state is registered: both in his own laughter and in the lion's 'gentle, protracted roar', which is the sign that his children are near.[30]

This concern with the quality of the voice recurs throughout Nietzsche's writing in relation to specifically philosophical creativity. On this point, the affects of the philosopher of the future overlap with those of certain kinds of artist. Thus, Zarathustra implores his soul to sing, as Nietzsche later wished his own soul had done in writing *The Birth of Tragedy*. It is a question of the relation that a particular philosopher-artist has to his or her work. A spirit that is unsure of itself, uncertain of its own power or of the character of its product will become agitated, breathe heavily, and speak too loudly or with too much haste. This is the fate of those who think against the grain of the culture in which they live. By contrast, 'a spirit that is sure of itself . . . speaks softly; it seeks concealment, it keeps people waiting'.[31] The perception of Nietzsche as a philosopher who speaks loudly is based in part upon the opening speeches of Zarathustra, where he appears as the prophet of thunderclouds and lightning. But in this form Zarathustra fails to make himself understood and must be metamorphosed, firstly into the silent convalescent conversing with his soul and then into the final figure, 'glowing and strong', who awaits the arrival of his children. Zarathustra himself has to learn that 'it is the stillest words which bring the storm. Thoughts that come on doves' feet guide the world.'[32] In fact, these words are spoken not by Zarathustra but by the nameless something which speaks to him, 'voicelessly', in his stillest hour, at the end of Book II. It is as though Nietzsche's most profound philosophical thoughts, the subtlest and most wicked thoughts, were spoken in a voice of such profound quietness that it is hardly a voice at all.

SOCIAL SPACE

As a maternal body, the philosopher-artist is characterised by a degree of antipathy to the public sphere of social life, to the 'masculine' sphere of commerce or worldly affairs. The maternal instinct of the philosopher, Nietzsche suggests, 'the secret love of that which is growing in him, directs him toward situations in which he is relieved of the necessity of thinking of himself . . .'[33] Among the primary requirements for the optimum conditions of this type of existence are freedom from the compulsion of daily routine, from work other than one's own, from disturbance and noise of any kind, especially that associated with the clash of ambitions or the competition of the marketplace. Nietzsche's conception of the philosopher-artist would therefore seem to require the kind of solitude to which Zarathustra always returns, where he has only his mountain and his animals for company. Does this mean that the philosopher is by nature unsuited to urban environments, that for these rare animals 'it is bad to live in towns'?[34]

There is a widespread experience of nineteenth century urban life according to which the city is indeed the scene of great noise and disturbance. This experience is well documented in Marshall Berman's book, *All That is Solid Melts Into Air*,[35] and represented in Nietzsche's own derogatory comments on modern bourgeois life. All of the things which the creative philosopher-artist must necessarily shun are found here in abundance: the pursuit of wealth, sensual pleasure and the lust for certain kinds of power. According to Berman, the whirlpool of urban existence gives rise to the very inner chaos which makes the modern soul so restless and constantly distracted, so incapable of settling upon a single goal to which to devote its energies. However, this experience of the city as a maelstrom shows its age. It is at best an early modern experience that we no longer share, or one that only ever occurred to those on the point of transition from the slower and more regular rhythms of rural life to the 'disorder' of newly formed urban existence. For late twentieth century urban dwellers, the city is no longer, or only occasionally, experienced as chaos. For the most part, urban life has acquired its own relatively stable routines. We experience it through the more or less integrated assemblages of work and transport systems; educational, recreational and political institutions. Individual lives tend to function along sub-routines no less regular than those of pre-modern social life, even if at more variable speeds. People tend to have their own more or less stable trajectories of work and play. Solitude is always an option. The 'stable, calm lines' on the horizon of one's life, without which the soul becomes distracted and which Nietzsche thought could only be found in the lines of mountain tops or trees[36] can now be discerned in tall city buildings, the sweep of expressways and the graceful climb and descent of jets on flight paths.

In any case, Nietzsche's diagnosis of the universal haste of modern life is the inverse of Berman's. It is not that movement kills thought but rather that the absence of thought leads to the increased velocity of social life. In a period in which the highest values have become devalued, individuals lack the resources to reflect on their lives. They are in perpetual flight from their own emptiness. The philosopher-artist has the capacity to create new values, but requires solitude in which to do so. The primary affect which characterises his or her relation to social space is not a will to confrontation but a 'will to the desert'. While this does not exclude flight from the city, it is not really a question of geography so much as of moral and social cartography. The philosopher of the future will be a 'wanderer', a transient who abjures attachments to existing institutions and ideas, but the desert in which he or she wanders is primarily a smooth space in the manner of Deleuze and Guattari's rhizome: that is, a mobile space characterised by the variable directions and the multiple dimensions in which movement is possible. It is a space in which we can move with a freedom limited only by our capacity to create new bodies, by our power to impose new forms of movement against the forces of capture and stratification.

To find such a space may require a degree of effacement before one's social milieu, a becoming-invisible which can be created as readily in an urban as in a rural setting: 'A voluntary obscurity perhaps; an avoidance of oneself; a dislike of noise, honor, newspapers, influence; a modest job, an everyday job, something that conceals rather than exposes one . . .'[37] Above all, what is absent from this desert is noise, where 'noise' must be understood in the sense of redundant information: everything that importunes the artistic spirit and distracts it from its own song. Even a song that is too loud may be noise, as Life herself tells Zarathustra after his Second Dance

Song: 'Noise kills thought'.[38] The spirit that is sure of itself speaks softly, while the creative philosopher-artist reveres 'everything in the face of which the soul does not have to defend itself and wrap itself up—what one can speak to without speaking *aloud*.'[39]*

* An earlier discussion of some of the matters raised in this paper was published in *Praxis M*, 24, September 1989. I am indebted to Moira Gatens for many conversations on these issues, and for her careful reading and comments on this paper. My remarks on power have also benefited from comments by Carole Pateman on another paper dealing with that concept, and from my reading of her own work. I would also like to thank David Simpson for his helpful comments.

CATHRYN VASSELEU

5 Life itself

Among the many innovations in medical imaging technology which have occurred in the past few decades, one of the most remarkable has been the endoscope. The modern era of endoscopy is considered to have begun with the description, in 1958, of a flexible fiberoptic tube which enabled hitherto inaccessible inner reaches of the human body to be visualised *in vivo*.[1] Not surprisingly, the idea captured the popular imagination. For example, in the 1966 science fiction film *Fantastic Voyage*,[2] a miniaturised medical team (which includes Raquel Welch) is injected into the body of a dying scientist, and travels through $3 million worth of constructed sets whose anatomical accuracy had been authorised by supervising doctors. Director Richard Fleischer said that he wanted his film to 'inspire young people to some understanding of the incredible complexity of the human body and the sheer wonder of it.'[3]

A more recent development has been Electronic Video Endoscope (EVE),[4] which differs from the fiberoptic endoscope in that it contains a tiny light-sensitive TV camera attached to the tip of the endoscope. Illumination is provided by a glass-fibre bundle. The image travels as an electronic signal through the endoscope, and is converted into an image on a TV monitor. The video endoscope is not held to the eye like a traditional camera, but operated under the guidance of the TV monitor image. Depending on the procedure, the patient may be looking on (and sometimes with such fascination that no sedation may be needed).[5]

The term endoscopy encompasses a number of different medical procedures. For example, gastroscopy visualises the upper digestive tract, sigmoidoscopy visualises the lower digestive tract, and laparoscopy visualises the organs which can be accessed via a puncture through the navel. Apart from being used for the internal visualisation of the body for medical diagnostic evaluation and therapeutic intervention (perhaps most notably in *in vitro* fertilisation procedures performed on women), images obtained by endoscope techniques have been used with great effect in various documentaries to bring us face to face, so to speak, with the immediacy of the body's interior.

In one of the best known of these documentaries, *The Miracle of Life*,[6] the commentary includes the following claim:

> . . . what really happens in the biological microworld that a human being is created in still remains one of the secrets of life. In this programme we're able to reveal for the first time, some of these secrets, through pictures that are also unique, because they're based entirely on material from human organs and human tissues.

On the one hand, the endoscope is one of many medical instruments whose genealogy can be traced to the dissecting anatomical gaze of Andreas Vesalius.[7] Casting aside all ideality of the body's formal appeal, this mode of seeing incised right into the fabric of flesh in order to disclose, by means of light, the minutest detail of its vital function. On the other hand, anatomy was traditionally a morbid practice carried out under the curtain of night which life paradoxically threw over the body's inner workings. It was only death which opened the portals of the body to the light of day. To quote Foucault: 'Nineteenth century medicine was haunted by that absolute eye that cadaverizes life, and rediscovers in the corpse the frail, broken nervure of life.'[8] From a teleological perspective, the endoscope triumphs over this tradition of the morbid anatomist by dispatching the curtain of night. Enlightenment comes as sight, and the point in nature and the thing itself appear to touch each other[9] in the illumination of life itself.

But let's get this thing into perspective. The endoscope is one example from a revolution in medical imaging techniques which has coincided with the introduction of computer and video technology for visualisation and interpretation of the body by means of a screened digital image. Through the endoscope, the body's unknown volume unfolds as a framed and flattened topography. It is rendered as a surface over which purchase may be gained by the viewing subject. In the endoscope's action of screening an image, can be read a desire for purchase reminiscent of the camera obscura, whose images not only entertained but put things in perspective.

Developments in endoscope techniques employ an equation between the retinal image and the screen (an equation which has been much explored in photographic and film practices).[10] The body can be viewed by putting an eye to the camera, or from a screened image obtained through a camera in the instrument's tip. From a Cartesian perspective the apparatus of endoscopy reiterates not only that a picture, or an infinite series of pictures, stands between the world and the subject's perceptions of it. The claim is also made that optical images have an existence independent of the observer.[11] The endoscope image becomes an objectively won 'picture' or spatial metaphor for flesh which is otherwise hidden in darkness from our gaze.

In biomedical investigation, this 'spatial metaphor' is regarded as an intermediary image of 'the primary actuality of a natural organized body.'[12] This was Aristotle's first definition of the *intrinsic principle* of living things. It is also worthwhile to note Aristotle's observation that: 'Nature proceeds little by little by little from things lifeless to animal life in such a way that it is impossible to determine the exact line of demarcation, nor on which side thereof an intermediate form should lie.'[13]

Needless to say, many definitions of life have been proposed: the pre-Socratic models of water, air and fire; Plato's imposed life-soul; life as self-replicating form in Aristotle's work; and the models proposed by the amalgamists, atomists, mechanists, moleculists and vitalists, to name a few. Contemporary science reiterates Aristotle's diagnosis of an impossible line of demarcation—a line now fragmented and disseminated in an ever-proliferating array of different indeterminate life-forms, from cyborgs and artificial intelligence to computer viruses, frozen sperm and transgenic animals.

While the sovereignty and objectivity of the biological sciences has been challenged from many quarters, 'life' remains a fundamental if arbitrary present in virtually all critiques. In Husserl's phenomenological displacement of the object of knowledge by what he refers to as a preobjective, or prescientific, sphere of lived experience, this prescientific sphere is grounded in the *a priori* of the life-world. The prescientific world is a cultural world—'nothing more than a garb of ideas thrown over the world of immediate intuition and experience, [over] the life-world . . .'.[14] The results of science have their 'foundation of sense in this immediate experience and its corresponding world and refers back to it'.[15] Even when the empirical world has been suspended, there is still a *life*, or living present, which is the essence of all experience, meaning and objective scientific truth.

Here, models and images serve a metaphoric role—where metaphor is a mediator which translates and refers to that which precedes and escapes reduction to any thing. This significance of metaphor in scientific endeavour has been the subject of various phenomenological critiques, including Bachelard's phenomenotechnology. In this account, the objects of science are not natural phenomena given to us directly by an independent reality. They are instead *materialisable concepts* constructed by a range of instrumental practices that define the field of historical truth. Metaphor plays a pedagogical role in this endeavour, as a *metapoetics* which works towards illustrating new concepts, rectifying concepts, or even revealing a concept as a bad metaphor.[16]

However, without the assistance of idealised figures (such as the circle in geometry) the life sciences must also somehow figure the concept prior to and in the absence of metaphor if they aspire to scientific concepts. As Derrida has pointed out, the metaphor of a concept is dependent on a concept of metaphor.[17] The rectification of the concept by the dismissal of that which is, after all, 'only a metaphor', 'only a model', 'only an illustration', plunges the concept back into the pre-scientific rhetorical world. Caught, as the life-sciences are, within this world of intuitive images, there remains the *presence* of something which is hidden from us. What is covered, what is hidden in all this which is only an image is—*life*—the dissimulated focal point of all metaphor, which cannot be seen and thus demands metaphor.[18]

But the significance of metaphor does not end there. In *The Psychoanalysis of Fire*, Bachelard tries to illustrate what he calls 'a state of mind which fully *realizes* the most insignificant metaphors.'[19]

> Nowadays, since the scientific mind has changed structure several times, it has become accustomed to such numerous transpositions of meaning that it is less often a victim of its own expression. All the scientific concepts have been *redefined*. In our conscious lives we have broken off direct contact with the original etymologies. But the prehistoric mind, and *a fortiori* the unconscious, does not detach the word from the thing. If it speaks of a man as being full of fire, it wills something to be *burning* in him.[20]

The distinction which Bachelard is making here is between a scientific mind whose thoughts are tied to an historically determined scientific spirit, and a prehistoric mind or unconscious which is a natural given. This mind's thoughts are entirely intuitive and stand before historical determination. The subject is split between these two modes of thought. On the one hand, Bachelard emphasises that rationality and scientific spirit are not immutable. On the other hand, he undertakes a form of 'psychoanalysis' for 'blanching if not erasing, naive images'[21] in the interests of exposing the unavowed motives which confuse scientific understanding.[22] Intuitions are epistemological obstacles to systematic thought—'When we turn inwards upon ourselves we turn aside from truth.'[23]

But, while Bachelard stresses the historical arbitrariness of scientific truths, he also emphasises the formative power and *real*-ising effects of intuited metaphors—of metaphors that can fill a man's belly with fire. This *real*-ising effect is achieved through a process of assimilation. Taking fire and life as an example (fire is life, life is a fire), this assimilation is enacted through the metonymic equation of reciprocal metaphors, spark and seed, which are treated as both like and same:

> At the source of this assimilation, there is, we believe, the impression that the spark, like the seed, is a small cause which produces a great effect ... Through the interplay of in-extricable reciprocals, the seed is the spark and the spark is the seed ... When the two intuitions are linked together as these are, the mind believes it is *thinking*, even though it is moving only from one metaphor to another ... they have no real foundation, but simply rest upon one another.[24]

However, within Bachelard's metaphorology, spark and seed *do* share the same foundation, but only from the objective perspective of the scientific mind. That foundation is life, whose power of dissimulation allows it to escape mastery. With the shift to an objective perspective, the assimilation of a life of metaphors shifts to the dissimulation of life *in* metaphors. No wonder that Bachelard notes, with some bemusement, that fire, that striking immediate object, is *no longer a reality for science.*

> In the course of time the chapters on fire in chemistry textbooks have become shorter and shorter. There are, indeed a good many modern books on chemistry in which it is impossible to find any mention of flame or fire ... When, as I have done on many occasions, one asks educated persons and even eminent scientists, 'What is fire?', one receives vague or tautological answers which unconsciously repeat the most ancient and fanciful philosophical theories.[25]

Bachelard's work can be read as a description of the way in which scientific knowledge attains a metaphysical stature in the hidden life of metaphor—a hidden life whose essence it then proceeds to conjure. To quote Nietzsche:

> Do you really believe that the sciences would ever have originated and grown if the way had not been prepared by magicians, alchemists, astrologers, and witches whose promises and pretensions first had to create a thirst, a hunger, a taste for *hidden* and *forbidden* powers? Indeed, infinitely more had to be *promised* than could ever be fulfilled in the realm of knowledge.[26]

By metaphor we make things *sensible*, that is, both figures of the senses and meaningful figures in an abstract sense. As Derrida has made much of, there is both profit and loss in metaphoric force. It is in our interest that involvement with metaphor promises more than it gives.[27] And my argument is that not only philosophy but also science profits from this loss. My point is not that there is metaphor in the text of science, but that in the very manufacture of metaphors, images, models, diagrams and analogies, and their simultaneous dismissal as just substitutes for or illustrations of the essential thing, science effaces itself as a figurative practice. Science doesn't *need language* to convey the concepts of the *physikos*. Scientific practice *is* writing. It makes thing up. Its figurative strategies are constitutive of the objects whose essence they describe and its knowledges are textual and intertextual. I will return to the endoscope for an example.

The Miracle of Life includes some remarkable footage obtained through special endoscope techniques. At one point on the screen, there is a pale disc moving through a passage. The commentary orients our curiosity, not only towards what we see, but to the very fact that we are seeing it: 'Now we're looking directly inside the infundibulum's wondrous hilly landscape . . . and now the ovum has reached the fallopian tube tunnel, which *in reality* [my emphasis] is only several millimetres wide.'[28]

Is it the cinematic effect of unprecedented *realism*, supposedly achieved by suspending the distinction between representation and imaginary reality, which is being flaunted in these images? Or are we drawn in by the voyeuristic pleasure of peeping through a keyhole at flesh which is otherwise hidden from our gaze? (One could certainly excavate a wealth of phallic imagery in the endoscope as an over-endowed scopic instrument or organ, if one was interested.)

Neither explanation seems appropriate. One feature which remains unaccounted for is the emphasis on innovative display, revelation, the *aesthetic of astonishment* detected by Tom Gunning in the compulsion which gripped early cinematographers—the French Lumière brothers and Edison's Vita-graph Company in America. Here, in the oscillation between belief and incredulity, as still projections become endowed with animation, emphasis falls on the presentation of life as an *ungraspable phantom.*[29]

The experiencing of images obtained with the endoscope seems closer to the spirit of this aesthetic of astonishment than to realism. Making visible something which could not exist otherwise, making a play of appearances which confound the expectations of logic and experience, testing the limits of an intellectual disavowal—this is the scope of the endoscope. I know that my eyes cannot be turned inwards, and yet, through an eye that blazes within my body, I see the dark inside displayed before me. There is a moment of vertigo as the familiar limits of one's world view are recast by the power of a visual illusion. In this respect, these images participate in the traditions of the cinema of attractions. To quote Tom Gunning again:

> The cinema of attractions solicits a highly conscious awareness of the film image engaging the viewer's curiosity. The spectator does not get lost in the fictional world and its drama, but remains aware of the act of looking, the excitement of curiosity and its fulfillment . . . This cinema addresses and holds the spectator, emphasizing the act of display.[30]

What is often ignored in scientific images is the element of curiosity they play upon. They fascinate not only by imparting truths but by making a display of seeing as the avenue of revelation. The current obsession in medical diagnostic techniques, with digitalisation and visualised display of everything from heart-beat patterns to functions of the brain, is just one example. The popular fascination with images generated through fractal geometry is another. If you can visualise a shape, if you can *simulate* an object, you can, supposedly, understand it.[31] The slogans which are used to sell endoscopes include 'Seeing is believing', 'Discover the superior image' and 'The symbol of medical progress.'[32] Biomedical practices have transformed the pixel. This basic unit of the video screen has become the 'pic(ture)-cell'—the basic unit of the screened body in the new vitagraph technologies.

What I am drawing attention to here is the play of realism and of illusion in scientific images. This play shifts the emphasis of scientific images from the revelation of physical reality to the materialisation of phantoms. The human ovum seen through the endoscope is not simple a copy—a model of the *same*, or thing from which the resemblance of the copy derives. It is a simulacrum, an image which is essentially a perversion of the possibility of resemblance. The simulacrum includes within the lure of its implied depth a differential point of view—an angle which incorporates the spectator as part of its dissimulation. The power of the simulacrum lies in the production of an effect through the *simulation* of likeness.[33]

It is possible to analyse the genealogy of the human ovum as an effect of such simulation. The empirical practices known as the life sciences, do not, I am arguing, deal with material which is already constituted as living, but brute matter. The constituted object and the constitutive act are inseparable in the life sciences as in all other writing practices. There is ambivalence in all efforts of determination. Presence necessarily entails an element of alterity that can neither be excluded nor integrated into the thing itself, but is the condition of possibility of presence. The identification, or recognition, of any object involves two distinct but interdependent operations. To quote Samuel Weber:

> There must be contact made with something new, different, something other than what has previously been presented to our minds. But at the same time, for the process of identification to take place, for us to apprehend anything as a determinate object, as a 'this' and not a 'that', that something new must be assimilated, compared, put into relation to things already known, to the familiar.[34]

The re-cognition of the familiar is itself an intrinsically open-ended repetition of earlier perceptions, cognitions and interpretations—a process of apprehension by substitution which defies comprehension.

The genealogy of the human ovum can be traced to a marriage, conceived by Aristotle, between the *catamenia*, or formless material of retained menstrual flow, and the *pneuma*, or organising power in semen. This marriage formed the *proper egg*—'the name given to that class of perfected *fetation* [mix of male and female] out of which the forming animal comes into being'.[35] When, centuries later, William Harvey was unable to find any coital material or conception in the uterus of a deer for several days after it had been mated, he concluded that the eventual foetus must be the product of a latent ovum which materialised after coitus. This potential embodied in the ovum was therefore the condition of conception itself. It was a 'certain corporeal something having life in potentia'.[36] An aura emitted by semen was absorbed into the blood, thereby activating and actualising this potential of the ovum. Henceforth, all animals arose from an inherent primordium—the egg became the origin of all life. From here it became a matter of metaphor—of fleshing out that certain something which Harvey hadn't seen. According to later investigators, these eggs arose in the 'female testes'. 'We shall call these vesicles "ova"', wrote Regner de Graaf, of some tiny spherical objects he had seen in a rabbit's reproductive tract, 'on account of the exact similitude which they exhibit to the eggs contained in the ovaries of birds'.[37]

The ova made apparent by de Graaf's interpretations clearly invalidated Harvey's view. The ovum was no longer a body with a certain potential but *produce* of the female 'testes' or ovaries—an egg, exactly like a chicken's, except for the shell. Direct evidence of production was lacking until Karl Ernst von Baer's description of *ovulation*. This description animated the mammalian egg by establishing the presence of a hollow and transparent structure at a series of points plotted from the ovarian follicle along the oviduct and into the uterus. It had become apparent that de Graaf had mistaken the chicken for the egg, or rather, the follicle for the ovum. The *ova* he had recognised were now the ovarian, or Graafian follicles which produced them.

With the advent and institution of cell theory, the cellular ovum was discovered. Furthermore, it was discovered to be the body's largest cell. The essential premise of cell theory was that all tissues were cellular in origin. The cell was the basic unit of life, and I add by way of emphasising the metaphor here, cell in the sense of a beehive—the structural unit of cooperative enterprise. To quote Georges Canguilhem: 'Cell is a word which does not make us think of the monk or the prisoner, but the bee.'[38] While the definition of the cell is an issue which is still openly in dispute today, the new unity which the universalism of cell theory imposed on life's diversity also undermined the supposed specificity of the ovum.

Prior to cell theory, the egg's identity was determined in the dichotomy between semen/egg, form/matter, actual/potential, active/passive. By emphasising the similarity of all cells, cell theory temporarily disrupted this dichotomy. Once both eggs and semen were reduced to a common cellularity, there was basically no difference between them. Reproduction became an asexual affair.[39] The reinscription of sexually differentiated cells has been the task of modern cytology and genetics. By virtue of their chromosomes, sex cells now form an exceptional, and in essence, potentially immortal body, differentiated from, while supported by, 'the rest of the body' or transient somatic cells. The shell-less chicken egg has rematerialised as the infinitely manipulable soft-cell ovum of reproductive genetic engineering. Its profile—a decentred circle—is yet another metaphor of life in the postmodern age, whose ex-centricities include a battery of new and different forms of egg collection.

There have been a number of challenging critiques of reproductive theory[40] which argue that scientific narratives of fertilisation and sex determination traditionally have been modelled on the cultural patterns of male/female interaction (for example, the characterisation of the egg as sporting trophy, whore, bride, gang rape victim, and most recently, assertive woman choosing her mate). However, emphasis in these critiques falls on the cultural determination of autonomous living matter:

> Science is a creative human endeavour whereby individuals and groups of individuals collect data about the natural world and try to make sense of them. Each of the basic elements of scientific research—conceptualisation, execution and interpretation—involves creativity . . . Any creative enterprise undertaken by human beings is subject to the influences of society. It is not surprising, then to see how gender becomes affixed to cells, nuclei and even chemicals. Even the interpretations of mathematical equations change with time.[41]

Socially informed creative scientific practice in turn authorises the determination of cultural reality: 'A theory about life affects life. We become what biology tells us is the truth about life.'[42] Although this form of critique depicts science as a creative enterprise which throws a 'garb of ideas', to use Husserl's expression, over life, 'life' has an essential but culturally determined reality.

Historical analysis of scientific truths is used in these critiques to underscore the interpretive aspect of scientific practice. But while it is demonstrated that the determination of things *changes* historically, the constitutive dimension of scientific interpretation—the dimension which undermines the possibility of distinguishing between object and interpretation—is limited to the cultural, as opposed to *a priori* life-world. Interpreters of science as a cultural phenomenon have recognised that science has to some extent abandoned a teleological perspective and assumed a more historical one.[43] However, science and critiques of science will not abandon or examine the dual perspective of science. There is always an open aspect of things, amenable to the senses and cultural manipulation, and a hidden aspect of things—their life-source, knowable only by inference, theory or analysis. Science preserves 'life-itself' as a domain in need of constant reformulation by *it*. Science alone holds out the promise of negotiating the abyss which lies beyond *its* artefacts. And it holds out this promise in the lure of metaphors and images, which re-present and re-iterate the conjuring feats of science. What is not acknowledged in all this is that the hidden is never outside the text. Nor can science assume a locus of detachment or speculation which is not implicit in its own practice. Science is an interpretive practice which is inscribed by and in its own writing.

The 'living', or 'biological' body is an *a priori* which is the effect of an interpretive practice. It is only within and through biomedical science that this body has an essential figuration. To quote Francois Jacob: 'Like other sciences, biology today has lost many of its illusions. It is no longer seeking the truth. It is building its own truth.'[44] And for this reason biologistic arguments, that is, arguments which make assertions based on biological truths, can hold no more authority than the practices which make these truths.[45]

Biologism is a charge which can be reduced to the practices which give life to biology. There can be nothing fixed about the biological. Essence cannot reside in biology until and unless the biological has been constituted as an *a priori*. As has already been discussed, the appropriation and constitution of this given is the business and defining principle of the biomedical sciences. There are many texts of the body. The biological body is just one of these texts. Its determinations are textual strategies, or the realities of interpretation. To read the biological body as simply the essential body is to ignore the essentialising function of writing, and, in this instance, the body-writing practices of biomedical science.

Scientific images are not merely a form of photo-graphy; they participate in vita-graphy. The ovum is not inscribed material. It is an effect of inscription which in turn has inscribing effects. The egg which waits passively inside a body surfaces as the mark by which that body is read. Furthermore, the inscribed always implies something other than what appears; identity is referred elsewhere—it is undone in the very moment it is constituted. What appears as the truth of a body is the mark of the evasion of any coincidence. For a woman patient in an IVF clinic, the ovum being visualised on the screen, and collected with the assistance of laparoscopy, has all the reality of a metonymic assimilation. It is becoming part of the text which is her body.

ROSALYN DIPROSE

6 A 'genethics' that makes sense

This DNA, this double helix, this bare substance of our chromosomal being, source of our sameness, root of our difference.

Fay Weldon, *The Cloning of Joanna May*[1]

To be located in space, which we all are, and to locate others, which we all do, requires embodiment. To be positioned, and to take up a position (even if this involves sitting on the fence) is a question of ethics. 'Ethics' is derived from the Greek word *ethos*, meaning dwelling, or habitat—the place to which one returns. Habitat encompasses habits which, as the product of the repetition of bodily activities, make up one's 'character'—one's specificity or what is properly one's own.[2] To belong to, and project out from an *ethos* is to take up a position in relation to others. This involves comparison, relation to what is different and to what passes before us. Taking up a position, presenting oneself, therefore requires a non-thematic awareness of temporality and location. And, the intrinsic reference point for temporality, spatial orientation and, therefore, difference, is one's own body. That location and position are concepts easily interchangeable, illustrates the co-incidence of embodiment and ethics which necessarily come together by virtue of our spatio-temporal being-in-the-world.

To define ethics in terms of bodily specificity would seem to be at odds with a more modern understanding of ethics. We more usually understand ethics in terms of a universal set of principles which ought to govern behaviour, principles which are formulated and grasped by the rational mind. As these principles claim universality, they evoke an ethics which assumes that behaviour originates in a potentially unified mind housed in a broad, homogeneous habitat.

Despite this emphasis, there are some contemporary accounts of an ethics based on bodily specificity.[3] These variously locate the body as the site of one's habitat or subjectivity—where the body is constituted by a dynamic relation with other bodies in a social context of power, desire and knowledge.

The discrepancy between these two approaches to ethics is not simply a question of etymology. Related to this are different, and usually unacknowledged, understandings of the components which go to make up our spatio-temporal being-in-the-world. The difference pertains to whether we think 'being' is composed primarily of mind or matter; to what we understand by the relation between mind and matter; and to whether we think the world we inhabit is homogeneous or fragmented. Underlying all these questions is some assumption about the meaning of 'in'.[4] An ethics based on universal rational principles assumes that our 'being' is a discrete entity separate from the 'world' such that we are 'in' the world after the advent of both. An ethics of bodily specificity, on the other hand, claims that our 'being' and the 'world' are constituted by the relation 'in'.

Science, that field of knowledge which governs the formulation of the nature of our being and the world we are 'in', assumes the first relation—that our 'being' and the 'world' are primordially distinct. And, as scientific descriptions of the body and the 'world' the body inhabits are thought to hover above both without effect, then ethics is thought to have no place in knowledge.

Despite this distancing and despite a privilege given to an ethics based on universal rational principles, the increasing public scrutiny of the activities of biomedical science suggests a link between science, the specificity of embodiment and ethics. The link is suggestive only. Much of the recent discussion around biomedical ethics does move away from abstract, formal principles, stressing instead individual rights, particular contexts and specific needs.[5] However, the nature of being and individuality is usually assumed in these discussions and rarely is there any analysis of *how* or *why* medicine and science, as modes of knowing, are necessarily ethical. What is even more surprising, given the material of biomedicine, is that rarely is any explicit reference made to the significance of embodiment to biomedical ethics.

David Schenck's paper, 'The Texture of Embodiment: Foundation for Medical Ethics', is a notable exception.[6] Schenck, following Merleau-Ponty, acknowledges that the body is 'our centre of activity in the world'.[7] As we comport ourselves towards the world *through* our bodies then, he argues, our body is not just an instrument by which we express ourselves. Rather, the body '*is literally our selves expressed*'.[8] Biomedical science and medical practice are by nature ethical because they deal with our most intimate and alienating possession—the body as our mode of social expression:

> It is the texture of bodily being that gives to medicine as social practice and medical ethics as social discourse their particular and distinctive features . . .[9]

At the same time, Schenck limits the ethics of medicine to its role of intervention after the texture of the body, its social 'expressiveness', has been rendered incoherent:

> Medicine deals with the *brokenness* of the body. . . . The collapse of the body at once invites and necessitates care by others. It *invites* care by virtue of the social expressiveness of the body, the call the injured body makes to unimpaired others . . . [W]hat is given over to others in these moments is that which is most intimate to one's self, most important to one's presence in the world.[10]

Schenck recognises that the basis of our specific being-in-the-world is our particular embodiment. And he locates medical ethics in the responsibility involved in *repairing* that being-in-the-world. His analysis, therefore, suggests an ethics of difference—one that recognises the material significance of embodiment to subjectivity. However, the connection he makes between 'being' and 'world' remains unclear and 'in' takes on the status of the copula. It would seem that our 'being', while bodily and habitual, only encounters the 'world' it inhabits after it is constituted. And, as biomedical practices only make the body their object after it is 'broken', then they are included in the 'world' that our being encounters. By separating our 'being' from the social discourses and practices which make up the 'world', Schenck's analysis seems to beg the question of *how* the body is the self expressed. What is it, if not something about the 'world', that constitutes the significance of our bodily specificity? What constitutes the habitat/habits which hold together the specificity of our being? While providing an astute analysis of the bodily foundation of medical ethics, Schenck not only leaves these questions unanswered, but seems to contradict the tradition of thought upon which his analysis depends.

Merleau-Ponty, for example, claims that the body, which is the bearer of orientation or position, is not 'in' the world after the advent of both: 'our body is not primarily *in* space: it is of it'.[11] Similarly, Heidegger argues that our being is not 'in' the world in the way water is in a glass. Rather, our 'being-in' is constituted by the context of meaningful relations with which we are involved.[12] We can only 'dwell' in a world, encounter objects within it and be encountered as an object (say, by science) if we are constituted by a set of relations with which we are, thereby, 'familiar'. This 'familiarity', and the world's significance, is governed by a non-thematic pre-ontological 'understanding' of Being. For Merleau-Ponty, this pre-reflexive understanding resides in the body's orientation activity; for Heidegger, it resides in a history which we cannot control but which presents us as we evoke it at every moment. For both, the objectifying practices which represent our being (including biomedical science), are secondary modes of 'understanding'. But, as such, they do constitute a particular mode of existence—one which marks a border between a human being and the world it inhabits. If Schenck is to follow this tradition, then he would need to recognise that biomedical science has a role in the constitution of our being as a discrete entity and is not just a mode of reparation of that being.

Biomedical science does not, of course, confess to any constitutive role in the specificity of our embodiment. It does acknowledge a role in the observation and manipulation of that specificity and takes on some responsibility for ensuring that its manipulative function is not socially detrimental. This distinction between the making of the body and its manipulation is maintained by a division between theory and practice. That is, biomedical science claims to 'know', at least potentially, the elements and intricate processes which go together to make up a particular body. It also claims to 'know' in what ways, and for what reasons, bodies differ. This theoretical mode of biomedical science delineates the source of the specificity of our embodied being—a specificity thought to lie outside that mode of knowing. On the other hand, biomedical practice can *alter* the texture of the body. Only as this secondary mode of intervention, does biomedical science claim a constitutive role—in its ability to modify human matter.

Nowhere is biomedical science more active in its description and manipulation of bodily specificity, and nowhere are the distinctions between observing and doing, theory and practice, fact and value, knowledge and ethics more pronounced, than in the field of genetics. An excursion into the debate about the ethical issues surrounding modern genetics best reveals what is problematic about these distinctions for an ethics aimed at enhancing our being-in-the-world.

Through an increasingly vigorous and public debate about the ethics of genetics, we have been asked to share in the geneticist's competence as well as in the responsibility for the always uncertain consequences of scientific research. The reason why genetics is now thought to require the critical attention of all of us is best summarised in the following terms by one exemplary account: 'Genetics, perhaps more than any other branch of science except brain biology, probes deeply into the identity of individual human beings'.[13] Any account of modern genetics will describe how a cell's genetic content determines its metabolic processes and physical appearance. We are thus given some insight into how and why geneticists think that genes are ultimately responsible for a body's functioning and appearance and, ultimately therefore, its identity and difference.

These accounts also usually include some critical assessment of the practical application of genetic theory. The potential for designer bodies or 'gene therapy'—the 'insertion', 'modification' and 'substitution' of genetic material to correct 'defects'—is a common cause for concern. But the application of genetics is not limited to its potential for eugenics. Genetic theory informs a wide range of social and medical practices. It is the condition for the possibility of immunological theory which in turn informs the approach to diseases such as AIDS.[14] Genetics also underscores screening for 'defective' individuals such as the criminal (through 'DNA fingerprinting', for example) or a foetus carrying a genetically transmitted disease. Reproductive technology, the development of biological weapons and the selective breeding of flora and fauna for agricultural production all owe their vigour, splendour and status to modern genetics.

Not all genetic practice is considered to be of ethical significance and, even when caution is advised, not everyone agrees.[15] The ethical import of genetics seems to depend, in the first instance, upon the degree to which *modification* or manipulation of bodily specificity is involved. Why this matters to the guardians of science is usually expressed in the following terms: '. . . biomedical engineering circumvents the human context of speech and meaning, bypasses choice and goes directly to work to modify the human material itself.'[16] By evoking a distinction between 'social meaning' and matter (which allows the distinction between knowledge, or observation, and intervention), such arguments claim that biomedical manipulation can institute an irreversible change to one's habitat. This implies that other vehicles of social change (the 'alteration of meaning' for example) are more flexible. Also, that there is an original and 'pure' mode of being which, presumably, resides outside of 'social meaning' in nature.

Not all genetic practice involves manipulation of matter—sometimes it is just a matter of surveillance. But surveillance, or genetic screening, and genetic engineering share a second feature considered to be of ethical import: a certain attitude about difference. Nobody wants to create a chimera (at least no one would admit to this)—the fantastic is considered to be too perverse, too offensive to our sensibilities. Rather, as Leon Kass has suggested, both the supporters and opponents of genetic engineering have, from the time the dream began, 'ground their hopes and their fears in the same prospect: *that man can for the first time re-create himself*'.[17] This desire to double the self, by reproducing the self or making the other the same, is the target of concern about the role of genetic screening and manipulation in the eradication of difference.

The preservation of diversity is the primary concern expressed by David Suzuki and Peter Knudtson in their account of modern genetics in *Genethics*. They cite numerous examples of applied genetics which 'intentionally' or inadvertently seek to eliminate the expression of difference. The Human Genome Initiative (HGI)—a project aimed at mapping the 100 000 or so genes in the human genome—is a less obvious case in point. HGI expresses the hope of locating all genes responsible for disease, normal metabolic processes and subtle hereditary differences between individuals. With this prospect, Suzuki and Knudtson caution against the possibility of establishing 'wholescale genetic screening programs ... for identifying individuals who harbor genes considered "defective" or "inferior"'.[18] Such programs, they claim, place too much confidence in a direct causal link between genes and individual behavioural differences and could result in misguided attempts to normalise and/or isolate individuals considered to be inferior.

There is little doubt that modern genetics lends authority and sophistication to the practices which map and attempt to efface differences. Yet, as the champions of genetics will point out, we have at our disposal more efficient means to 'regulate human behaviour' and minimise the expression of difference.[19] Any sinister use of genetics, they argue, reflects the contamination of science by the ideology governing these other means of regulation. This may be the case. But the defence of genetics here again relies on a distinction between 'social meaning', or a biased interpretation of differences, and differences *per se*. Even Suzuki's and Knudtson's caution implies this distinction by separating theory from practice and then questioning the ability to interpret the meaning and value of observed differences without reference to an unsubstantiated social norm. What supposedly marks 'pure' genetics off from 'other' methods of social regulation, and from the 'bad politics' which may allow its misuse, is that its authority is derived from the claim to know the origin of the expression of difference outside its 'social meaning'. Presumably then, the ethically correct categorisation and manipulation of bodily specificity in the practical application of genetics would involve, not the social evaluation of difference in terms of a social norm, but reference to the origin of difference *per se*.

Implied in these warnings about the evaluation of difference is a claim that this evaluation is relational and therefore should be avoided. But, as Hegel reminds us, identity (in this case, one's bodily specificity) is *produced* through differential relations.[20] To label something or someone defective or inferior relies on the assumption that the 'proper' stands alone. Yet, some notion of the proper as sameness does silently underscore the evaluation of difference with real effects. And, it does so by the institution of an interval between the one and the other. What constitutes this interval between entities is also what constitues the 'in' between one's being and the world. It is what prevents each identity from dissolving into its other (including the subject and object of knowledge). Genetics, by referring to the origin of difference, claims to know the nature of this interval—what lies between entities such that their difference is real. However, it is the complicity of genetics in the *production*, rather than the indifferent description, of this spacing which requires more attention. What I will argue below is that genetic theory is itself a genetic operation—it is involved in the production of difference in the terms of sameness. On the other hand, because the self comes into being in the other, both the subject and object of knowledge are always other than themselves. Hence, the genetic determination of bodily specificity is necessarily deferred.

Genetic theory takes place in a mode of existence which assumes a distinction between the subject and object of knowledge, between the specificity of our bodily being and the discourses which describe that being and make up the world we inhabit. So genetics, at the level of theory, is considered to have a representative rather than a constitutive function in its delineation of the origin and somatic expression of difference. It would seem that genetics, as theory, has no ethics—it does not make the sensory; it makes sense of the sensory. At least its aim is to make sense.

But could genetics make sense in another sense? As a branch of science, genetics promises absolute knowledge or the Truth of Being. Even if incomplete, there is still a promise of more complete and adequate truth. And, lurking within this promise is the same attitude about difference which is of concern in applied genetics. As Emmanuel Levinas claims: 'Without doubt, the finite being that we are cannot in the final account complete the task of knowledge; but in the limit where this task is accomplished, it consists in making the other become the Same.'[21] For Levinas, it is alterity which provokes the desire to know—a claim which seems obvious in the case of genetics. Yet, the subject of knowledge does not simply discover the nature of the interval between entities or between itself and its object. Rather, the subject of knowledge forms and transforms this interval by constituting the other in its own image. We may be sympathetic with the call to responsibility being made by the custodians of science towards the geneticist. But if the formative activity of applied genetics is informed by a similar distribution of difference at the level of theory then perhaps this 'finger pointing' is slightly misplaced.

If 'pure' genetics is a simple re-presentation of the origin and expression of difference then it must uphold its claim to be uncontaminated by 'social meaning' and be devoid of productive effects. But, every aspect of genetic theory is informed by the same notion of difference apparent in its practice. This is difference as complementarity. A notion which assumes a preferred identity and where the one and its other appear to stand apart before coming together to make a whole. Genetic theory, in this way, is remarkably reminiscent of the doubling of self of concern in applied genetics. As we accompany the geneticist to the origin of difference we encounter a neat coupling. Beginning with sexual difference we find that the man and the woman each contribute half the complement of chromosomes to be found in the cells of their offspring. These match up into 22 pairs plus two sex chromosomes (identical in females, different in males). Each chromosome consists of a DNA double helix containing two complementary strands which 'are related in much the same way as a photographic print and the negative from which it is made. Each harbors the shadowy image of the other.'[22] And each DNA strand is joined to the other via a series of nucleotide bases which will only link with their opposite.

Described in this way, one would assume that the microscopic distribution of differences mimics sexual difference, or the way in which we map sexual difference at the level of the social—as opposition and complementarity where the negative is the other side of a favoured image. But, according to the geneticist, the production of difference is the other way around: difference as complementarity at the macro-level is an expression of, and stops with, the genetic code. In other words, the genetic code grounds this mirroring effect and is what prevents each identity from dissolving into the other through its determination of difference in and for itself. At least, this is the case in theory. However, in the pathway between the genetic code and its expression there lies another slippery operation of difference and an unsuccessful attempt to contain difference as the other side of sameness. And, even the origin of difference, the gene, defies identification in itself.

While the gene is proposed as the origin of meaning, its expression is determined, not by a discrete code as one would assume, but by the *order* of nucleotide base pairs along the DNA double strand. Nor do contiguous relations alone determine the expression of difference. This sequence must first be replicated or 'transcribed' into the form of a mirror image of itself. This discordant doubling is then reversed: the message carried by the messenger is 'translated' back by specifying the production of its own mirror image. With the appearance of the other of the other, we don't return to the code from which we began: the bases which make up the transfer RNA carry with them the base units of proteins which dutifully assemble according to the order of their nucleotide base hosts—an order prescribed, via a detour through the other, by the 'original' code. With this synthesis of proteins the genetic message is expressed at the microscopic level. But the message must pass through a further symphony of differential relations before difference is orchestrated at the surface of the body. In a mysterious and unknown way the relation between proteins determines the function and shape of cells, the distribution of which determines the function and shape of different parts of the body and, hence, the morphology of the whole.

Even if the geneticist's map were complete, which it is not, the most it could explain is sameness from repetition, not difference. While this description of the origin and expression of difference indicates that the manifestation of the message is always other than itself, there is an attempt to contain the production of meaning within the paradigm of exact translation. This requires insisting, despite all indications to the contrary, upon an integrity between the code and its expression. And such integrity can only be claimed if the code is original, discrete and can, in its necessary passage through the other, completely subsume the other to itself without remainder. The cost of insisting on total incorporation is that diversity, which is the rule rather than the exception, tends to be understood in terms of disruption, breakdown or mutation in the process of transmission rather than an expression of an absence of integrity in re-production. It is therefore not surprising that difference in 'applied' genetics is understood in the same terms.

At the same time, the geneticist concedes, even within his or her own paradigm, that the expression of the code is never exact, nor is the code original. There is a play of difference which is the condition for the possibility of both the 'original' code and of the oppositional difference operating in its expression. For a start, the gene does not simply appear but is a product of a prior distribution of differences—sexual difference (meosis) and prior DNA replication—and is prone to the uncertainties of both. This uncertainty is acknowledged in genetics but is put down to the limits of knowledge rather than its effect—the effect of a process of signification which divides and disperses entities as it grounds and presents them.

The effect of attempting to contain difference within a notion of complementarity also manifests in the inability of genetics to explain adequately the process of DNA transcription and translation without the production of, and reference to, other 'outsides'. For instance, what prior 'message' draws a boundary around base sequences to indicate the beginning and end of a code? Other base sequences ('terminators' and 'promotors') 'which are not expressed', we are told. Who or what recognises these boundaries such that the process of transcription begins and ends appropriately? Enzymes determine this spacing. Who or what directs the work of enzymes? And there are further differential relations to which this no-longer-original code is referred, all of which are to account for a necessary ambiguity in the expression of meaning: the 'same' code is found in multiple locations; the activity of genes can be affected by the 'geographic location' of other genes; some genes are 'programmed' to be 'nomadic'; most genes are polymorphic and 'hereditary' differences are usually polygenic (involving the interplay of many genes). The spatio-temporal relations which determine the interplay of these different terms are said to be a product of yet another set of 'regulatory mechanisms'. But, of these, 'little is known'.[23]

While the mapping of difference which occurs in applied genetics is meant to be authorised by the truth of the origin of difference, we find that the 'origin' is always other than itself. The geneticist's dream of mapping the play of genes into a seamless whole will remain just that, a dream. This is because genetics does not re-present real differences; it signifies with material effects. As a mode of knowing which divides entities and claims their difference to be original and part of the same, genetics is itself a process of production of origins. This is a mode of production which Jacques Derrida would describe as a spacing which constitutes the interval, necessary for signification, between the two 'things' which that interval produces. It is a process which distributes differences only to ensure that the discrete identity of those differences is deferred. The genetic production of differences, therefore, guarantees the interruption of every self-identity.[24]

The search for the origin of identity and difference, therefore, cannot stop with the gene—an entity which the search itself produces. We are referred beyond genes to mysterious 'regulatory mechanisms' which oversee their production and spatio-temporal distribution. Nor will the origin be found there. As each origin dissolves into its other, we get closer to where we began: to the manifestation of differences at the surface of the body and between bodies, to their socio-political distribution and to the author of that distribution. However, we cannot find an ultimate author or subject of this system of differences either.[25] The geneticist, like the gene, is a placeholder, being also an effect of the same spacing and is, therefore, constituted only in being divided from itself. The body may be the self expressed, as Schenck would put it, but only with a lack of certainty—only by being inscribed in a system of differences which genetics helps to produce and maintain. In other words, we find that both the 'subject' and the 'object' of genetics, the 'world' and one's 'being', are constituted in relation to each other and are, therefore, always other than themselves.

The specificity of embodiment can be almost found in the thick of this genetics and is not indifferent to its terms. The production and manifestation of differences which genetic theory attempts to describe is not outside of that description: genetics is not simply an incorrect re-presentation of real differences. On the other hand, bodily differences cannot be reduced to the gene: genetics does not give us the truth of the origin of specificity. Rather, genetics is one particularly dominant mode of an infinite number of discursive practices which make differences real by the use of categories which produce and organise them through relations on the basis of sameness. The body is the homespun fabric of this process of organisation and, as such, it is an almost coherent, but somewhat fragile, effect of power and knowledge.

Genetics is included in what Michel Foucault refers to as biopower: the technologies of power deployed with the emergence of the modern biomedical and social sciences in the nineteenth century. Without reference to law, and without displaying themselves as power, these sciences divide and assemble the body, evaluate, sort and compare. They thereby transform life by effecting distributions around a norm.[26] The assumption of, and desire for, sameness pervade these sciences of the body. And, as I have argued, this urge to 're-create the self' informs genetic theory as well as its practice.

To the extent that the formative function of genetics is disavowed—its function of distributing differences in and between bodies—the body stands alone in the splendour of its presence. This spacing has material effects such that the body appears to stand apart from the 'world' or the discursive practices which constitute it and measure its difference as an apparent afterthought. At the same time, a body's specificity cannot be reduced to this objectification and the gap between our being and the world, which knowledge opens up, cannot be maintained. The origins and causes of being, which are the objects of knowledge, multiply in this gap. Just as the border of the gene disperses into a mirror image which exceeds it at the moment it is assembled, so does the border which marks off the body from the practices which objectify it. The knowledge which effects borders within and between bodies also provides the conditions for the possibility of their 'brokenness'.

If the specificity of embodiment, of one's *ethos* or habitat, is to be found anywhere, it is not in the work of some more archaic 'understanding' of Being nor in a unified identity which precedes the 'world'. Rather, it lies within the modes of knowing which present us by a spacing which simultaneously marks off as it interrupts every assemblage of self; in between a genetics which determines a body's difference in terms of a norm and the necessary deferment of that determination. One's *ethos* is marked by a *pathos*: by the conflicts and contradictions which are living testimony to the subjection of bodies to normalisation; to the impossibility of separating bodies from how they are known; and to the necessary disruption of both poles of this process of identification. It is marked by a somatic expression of difference referring to an 'original' code which cannot be found in and for itself; by a description of the operation of difference which refers to the same 'social meaning' or practice of distributing difference which it is meant to authorise or correct; by a genetics which owes its prestige to locating the source of bodily specificity but confesses only to locating sameness. These contradictions feed off and reinforce the conflicts which mark the specificity of embodiment in 'applied' genetics, both the glamour and shame of which derives from its normative function. Hence, a project such as HGI will, in attempting to map the origin of difference, effect and underscore the effacement of difference.

Attempting to locate a body definitively, or, taking up a position by evoking one's own specificity, necessarily involves reference to an 'outside'. Thus, conflict or a fundamental heterogeneity is disavowed at the moment it is produced. One's position is also one's dis-position. Genetics in theory or practice is complicit with this curious mode of production—it makes sense and non-sense, literally. So, medical ethics does not begin with its role in dealing with the 'brokenness' of bodies; nor does 'genethics' begin with the 'misuse' of theory in the practice of effacing differences. Biomedical ethics begins with the formative function of its own modes of knowing which, by mapping what remains other to oneself, are complicit with the constitution and dissolution of borders within and between bodies. Our ways of knowing are dependent upon and multiply differences which we then overlook. And in this production and effacement of different habitats we can locate the conditions for the possibility of what is considered 'unethical' practice. It would seem that biomedical science is an art in all its modes and, as Aldous Huxley claimed in his early warning about genetics, 'art also has its morality'.[27]*

* I would like to thank Robyn Ferrell and Cathy Vasseleu for their helpful comments on an earlier version of this paper. The research was conducted with the assistance of a fellowship from the American Association of University Women.

PART III
Of Bodies 2

MOIRA GATENS

7 Corporeal representation in/and the body politic

The rather awkward title of this paper is intended to draw attention to an ambiguity in the term 'representation' as it is used in political theory. First, I want to focus on the construction of the *image* of the modern body politic. This involves examining the claim that the body politic is constituted by a creative act, by a work of art or artifice, that uses the human body as its model or metaphor. The background to this claim is provided by certain seventeenth and eighteenth century social contract theorists who argued in favour of the conventionality or artificiality of monarchical political authority.[1] If such authority is neither natural nor God-given but rather based on agreement and convention then it is mutable. The way the metaphor of the body functions here is by analogy. Just as man can be understood as a representation of God's creative power, so the political body can be understood as a representation of man's creative power, that is, as *art(ifice)*.

The second sense of 'representation' surfaces when considering *whose* body it is that is entitled to be represented by this political corporation. This involves understanding 'representation' in the sense where one body or agent is taken to stand for a group of diverse bodies. Here we are considering the metonymical representation of a complex body by a privileged part of that body. The metaphor here slides into metonymy. The relevant background literature to this question is provided by various texts, from the seventeenth century on, concerning the natural authority of men over women and the propriety of taking the male head of households as representative of the concerns of the entire household.[2]

The first use of 'representation'—what I have called the metaphorical—concerns the way in which this image effects who is represented by the body politic. To address the first strand—the metaphorical—I will begin with a quotation from a mid-seventeenth century text that posits, in a manner typical of the period, a detailed correspondence between the parts and functions of the human body and the parts and functions of the political body. The text is the *Leviathan*, the author is Thomas Hobbes. He writes:

> by art is created that great LEVIATHAN called a COMMONWEALTH, or STATE, in Latin CIVITAS, which is but an artificial man; though of greater stature and strength than the natural, for whose protection and defence it was intended; and in which the *sovereignty* is an artificial *soul*, as giving life and motion to the whole body; the *magistrates*, and other *officers* of judicature and execution, artificial *joints*; *reward* and *punishment*, by which fastened to the seat of the sovereignty every joint and member is moved to perform his duty, are the *nerves*, that do the same in the body natural; and *wealth* and *riches* of all the particular members are the *strength*; *salus populi*, the people's safety, its *business*; *counsellors*, by whom all things needful for it to know are suggested unto it, are the *memory*; *equity* and *laws*, an artificial *reason* and *will*; *concord*, *health*; *sedition*, *sickness*; and civil war, death. Lastly the *pacts* and *covenants*, by which the parts of this body politic were at first made, set together, and united, resemble that *fiat*, or the *let us make man*, pronounced by God in the creation.[3]

I want to draw attention to two important aspects of the view Hobbes offers. First, Hobbes claims that the motivation behind the creation of the artificial man is the 'protection' or 'defence' of natural man. We may well wonder from whom or what natural man requires protection. Hobbes' answer is that he requires protection from other men and from nature. Man, in a state of nature, he tells us, is in 'continual fear' and in 'danger of violent death' and the quality of his life is summed up with the words 'solitary, poor, nasty, brutish, and short'.[4] The second thing I want to highlight is the *fiat*, the God-like pronouncement, that breathes life into the political body. For Hobbes this *fiat* refers to the pacts and covenants made by men between men. These demigods, whose speech has such awesome creative power, do not go on, in God-like fashion, to create an artificial Eve. Perhaps the sons can learn from the father's mistakes, after all.

The artificial man, a creation of 'the word' of men united, thus renders itself free from the necessary but difficult dealings with both women and nature. This masculine image of unity and independence from women and nature has strong resonances in psychoanalytic accounts of infantile anxieties and the fantasies created to cope with them.[5] The image of artificial man, the body politic, perfectly mirrors the infantile wish for independence from the maternal body. It is a fantasy that can be found in mythology too. Classical Athens, often considered to be the first true body politic, is named after Athena who was born not 'of woman' but 'of man': she sprang from the head of Zeus. Athens is named after Athena as a tribute to her for ridding that city of its 'uncivilised' divinities. When she relegates the feminine Furies to the subterranean regions of Athens, she confirms the masculinity of the Athenian political body. Like Hobbes' artificial man, she is the product of man's reason; she has no mother. Or has she? An often neglected part of this myth is that Zeus 'gave birth' to Athena only after he had swallowed whole the body of his pregnant wife.

In the absence of a female leviathan, natural woman is left unprotected, undefended, and so is easy prey for the monstrous masculine leviathan. Like the hapless Jonah, she dwells in the belly of the artificial man, swallowed whole, made part of the corporation not by pact, nor by covenant, but by incorporation. The modern body politic has 'lived off' its consumption of women's bodies. Women have serviced the internal organs and needs of this artificial body, preserving its viability, its unity and integrity, without ever being seen to do so.

The metaphor of the unified body functions, in political theory, to achieve two important effects. First, the artificial man incorporates and so controls and regulates women's bodies in a manner which does not undermine his claim to autonomy, since her contributions are neither visible nor acknowledged. Second, insofar as he can maintain this apparent unity through incorporation, he is not required to acknowledge difference. The metaphor functions to restrict our political vocabulary to one voice only: a voice that can speak of only *one* body, *one* reason, and *one* ethic.

Perhaps the metaphor of the human body is an obvious way of describing political life; so obvious that the metaphor passes into common usage, no longer mindful of its origins. If this is the case then perhaps it seems far-fetched to argue that the conception of the body politic is anthropomorphic. Yet, there is a sense in which the image of the polity is anthropomorphic if we limit this claim to a literal, or etymological, understanding of 'anthropos', which means 'man'. This leads me into the second strand of the use of 'representation' in modern political theory—the metonymical.

Here we need to consider *who* is represented by this image of bodily unity. Certainly not any human form, by virtue of its humanity, is entitled to consider itself author of or actor in the body politic. From its classical articulation in Greek philosophy, only a body deemed capable of reason and sacrifice can be admitted into the political body as an active member. Such admission always involves *forfeit*. From the original covenant between God and Abraham—which involved the forfeit of his very flesh, his foreskin—corporeal sacrifice has been a constant feature of the compact. Even the Amazons, the only female body politic that we 'know' of, practised ritual mastectomy.

At different times, different kinds of beings have been excluded from the pact, often simply by virtue of their corporeal specificity. Slaves, foreigners, women, the conquered, children, the working classes, have all been excluded from political participation, at one time or another, by their bodily specificity. Could the common denominator of these exclusions be 'those incapable of fulfilling the appropriate forfeit'? That is, those whose corporeal specificity marks them as inappropriate analogues to the political body. Constructing women as incapable of performing military service and so incapable of defending the political body from attack could serve as an example here. This incapacity, constructed or not, is sufficient to exclude her from active citizenship. At this level the metonymical aspects of the metaphor of the body function to exclude. Those who are not capable of the appropriate political forfeit are excluded from political and ethical relations. They are defined by *mere* nature, *mere* corporeality and they have no place in the semi-divine political body except to serve it at its most basic and material level. To explain how the metonymical aspects of the image of the body politic function to exclude it is necessary to examine this image of bodily unity in greater detail.

Discourses which employ the image of the unified political body assume that the metaphor of the human body is a coherent one, and of course it's not. At least I have never encountered an image of a *human* body. Images of human bodies are images of either men's bodies or women's bodies. A glance at any standard anatomical text offers graphic evidence of the problem with this phrase: 'the human body'. Representations of the human body are most often of the male body and, perhaps, around the borders, one will find insets of representations of the female reproductive system: a lactating breast, a vagina, ovaries; bits of bodies, body-fragments. They appear there in a way that reminds one of specialised pornographic magazines which show pictures of isolated, fragmented, disjointed bits: breasts, vaginas, behinds. Female-bits, fragments to be consumed, devoured a bit at a time.

This imaging has its correlate in political theory. Recent feminist work has shown that the neutral body, assumed by the liberal state, is implicitly a masculine body.[6] Our legal and political arrangements have man as the model, the centre-piece, with the occasional surrounding legislative insets concerning abortion, rape, maternity allowance, and so on. None of these insets, however, take female embodiment seriously. It is still the exception, the deviation, confined literally to the margins of man's representations. It is still 'anthropos' who is taken to be capable of representing the universal type, the universal body. Man is the model and it is his body which is taken for the human body; his reason which is taken for Reason; his morality which is formalised into a system of ethics.

In our relatively recent history, the strategies for silencing those who have dared to speak in another voice, of another reason and another ethic, are instructive. Here I will mention two strategies that seem to be dominant in the history of feminist interventions. The first is to 'animalise' the speaker, the second, to reduce her to her 'sex'. Women who step outside their allotted place in the body politic are frequently abused with terms like: harpy, virago, vixen, bitch, shrew; terms that make it clear that if she attempts to speak from the political body, about the political body, her speech is not recognised as *human* speech. When Mary Wollstonecraft, for example, had the audacity to address the issue of women's political rights,[7] Walpole called her a 'hyena in petticoats'. The strategy of reducing woman to her 'sex' involves treating her speech and her behaviour as hysterical. The root of 'hysteria' is the Greek 'hystera', meaning uterus. Disorder created by women, in the political body, is thus retranslated into a physical disorder thought to be inherent in the female sex.

Both these strategies insist on the difference between the image of the political body and the image of woman's body. However, it is a difference which is interpreted as evidence of woman's inadequacy in the political sphere. But, perhaps this difference no longer exists. After all, women are now admitted to the public sphere, they participate in politics, and sometimes, they even become Prime Ministers. However, to say this would be to miss the point. It is true that if women want to escape from the dreary cycles of repetition in the private sphere, then often they can. If they want to escape from the hysteria and mutism of domestic confinement, then often they can. But at what cost? We can be 'cured' of mere animal existence by 'becoming men'; 'cured' of hysteria by 'hysterectomy'.

I am willing to concede that the metaphor of the body politic is quite anachronistic and precariously anchored in present political and social practices. This body has been fragmented and weakened by successive invasions from the excluded: the slaves, the foreigners, the women, the working class; but this does not imply that we presently have a polymorphous body politic. Certainly, the last two to three hundred years have witnessed the removal of many formal barriers and formal methods of exclusion, but there is a lot more to be said about methods of exclusion than formalised principles of equity can address. If woman, for example, speaks from this body, she is limited in what she can say. If she lives by this reason and this ethic, she lives still from the body of another: an actress, still a body-bit, a mouth-piece.

It is not clear to me, taking into account the history of the constitution of this body politic, that it can accommodate anything but the same. I have suggested that the modern body politic is based on an image of a *masculine* body which reflects fantasies about the value and capacities of that body. The effects of this image shows its contemporary influence in our social and political behaviour which continues to implicitly accord privilege to particular bodies and their concerns as they are reflected in our ways of speaking and in what we speak about. It refuses to admit anyone who is not capable of miming its reason and its ethics, in its voice. Its political language has no vocabulary and no space for the articulation of certain questions. Our political body continues to assume that its active members are free from the tasks of reproduction, free from domestic work, free from any desires other than those 'whispered' to it by one of its Hobbesian 'counsellors' or 'willed' in it by one of its laws. All this body can address is questions of access to 'predefined' positions, and 'preconstituted' points of power or authority. It cannot address the question of *how* or in what manner one occupies these points or positions. Nor can it address the limiting conditions, dictated by the corporeal specificity of the occupant, on the possible actions open to that occupant. What it cannot address is how different bodies 'fill' the same 'empty' social or political space. I wonder, in this context, whether the withdrawal of Pat Schroeder from the US Presidential candidacy was related to this problem. She said, in her speech, that she was withdrawing because she could not 'figure out' how to occupy the political sphere without turning over her desires, behaviour and plans to predetermined meanings which were at odds with her own intentions.

I would suggest that this problem is, at least partly, related to the continuing fascination that we have for the image of the one body. It is an image that belongs to a dream of equity, based on corporeal interchangeability, that was developed to the full in nineteenth century liberalism. And it is a 'dream of men'. Women, and others, were not co-partners in this dream and to attempt to join it at this late stage is as futile as trying to share someone's psychosis. The socially shared psychosis of egalitarianism was constructed to deal with a specific problem: to diffuse the power structure of seventeenth and eighteenth century politics. This fantasy of the modern body politic, constituted by 'the word' of men united, is not appropriate to women, and others, who were specifically excluded from it. For these 'others', who have never experienced the satisfaction of having their image reflected back to themselves 'whole' or 'complete', the fascination with this dream is not so binding. The cultural ego-ideal was never something that they could live up to without a massive act of bad faith. But what are the alternatives?

If what one is fascinated by is the image of one body, one voice, one reason, any deviation takes the form of gibberish. If woman speaks from her body, with her voice, who can hear? Who can decipher the language of an hysteric, the wails of a hyena, the jabbering of a savage—apart from other hysterics, hyenas and savages? Our political vocabulary is so limited that it is not possible, within its parameters, to raise the kinds of questions that would allow the articulation of bodily difference: it will not tolerate an embodied speech.

The impotence of our political vocabulary leads me to suggest that the more appropriate sphere for a consideration of these questions may be the ethical. And here I am using 'ethical' in a sense perhaps long forgotten, where ethics is crucially concerned with the specificity of one's embodiment. It is certainly a pre-Kantian notion.[8] It is prior to the ever-narrowing *political* organisation of ethics and prior to the conceptualisation of ethics as reducible to a set of universal principles, dictated by reason (whose reason?). It is opposed to any system of ethics which elevates itself from a contingent form of life to the pretension of being the *one* necessary form of life. The most a universal ethic will permit is the *expansion* of the one body. Under pressure from its own insistence on equity, it may be forced to admit women, slaves, and others. It will not, however, tolerate the positing of a second, or a third, or a fourth body. Prime Minister Hawke's courting of the Aboriginal land rights movement prior to the Australian Bicentennial celebrations in 1988, could provide an example of my point here. He wanted to take the body politic off to the beauty-parlour so it would look its best for its big birthday party. An important component of this beauty-treatment involved attending to the blemishes on this body caused by the history of its abuse of Aboriginal bodies. It is instructive that Hawke wanted to 'make-up' by calling for a *compact*, a term that is more at home in seventeenth century political texts. The term carries connotations of an agreement between equals, between like beings, to join as a single body. Some Aborigines, on the other hand, called for a *treaty*, a term that carries connotations of an agreement between unlike beings to respect each other's differences. It also implies a demand for the recognition of *two* bodies. Hawke resisted a treaty because this would be to recognise another voice, another body, and this raises the deepest fears. To recognise another body is to be open to *dialogue*, debate and engagement with the other's law, and the other's ethics.

It seems important, if the possibility of dialogue and engagement is to be opened up, that feminist politics recognise the futility of continuing to ask to be fully admitted into this fantasy of unity. This would be to stop asking of that body that it be 'host', since for women this would be to ask how can I live off myself—how can I engage in self-cannibalism? I would rather want to raise the question: whose body is this? How many metamorphoses has it undergone? and what possible forms could it take? And in responding to these questions it seems crucial to resist the temptation, noticeable in some feminist writing, to replace *one* body with *two*, one ethic with two, one reason with two. For this would be merely to repeat, in dual fashion, the same old narcissistic fascination involved in the contemplation of one's own image. The most this will achieve is that we would succeed in throwing off the persona of Echo, who speaks but is not heard, only to join Narcissus at the pool.

Since this paper opened with a quotation that I take to be typical of a certain kind of male fantasy, I will also close with one. It comes from Italo Calvino's book, *Invisible Cities* which is constructed as a dialogue of sorts between Kublai Khan—the demigod State-builder, and Marco Polo—the inquisitive explorer who entertains Kublai Khan with accounts of the many cities he has seen. It is from a section entitled 'Cities and Desire'.

> From there, after six days and seven nights, you arrive at Zobeide, the White City, well exposed to the moon, with streets wound about themselves as in a skein. They tell this story of its foundation: men of various nations had an identical dream. They saw a woman running at night through an unknown city; she was seen from behind, with long hair and she was naked. They dreamed of pursuing her. As they twisted and turned, each of them lost her. After the dream they set out in search of that city; they never found it, but they found one another; they decided to build a city like the one in the dream. In laying out the streets, each followed the course of his pursuit; at the place where they had lost the fugitive's trail, they arranged spaces and walls differently from the dream, so she would be unable to escape again.
>
> This was the city of Zobeide, where they settled, waiting for that scene to be repeated one night. None of them, asleep or awake, ever saw the woman again. The City's streets were streets where they went to work every day, with no link any more to the dreamed chase. Which, for that matter, had long been forgotten.
>
> The first to arrive could not understand what drew these people to Zobeide, this ugly City, this trap.[9]

I take this dream to be rather atypical, for it tells of the failure of the desire to 'capture' and to 'contain' difference in a monument to unity. It also speaks of masculine impotence in the face of a loss suffered but not remembered. There is an interesting point of overlap between these dreams and fantasies of cities and states. The women of Zobeide are walled into that city just as surely as the Furies are contained in Athens. The possibility of hearing the speech of women and others, is crucially tied to the remembrance and 'working through' of this initial dream.*

* I would like to acknowledge the assistance given me by Rosalyn Diprose, Reta Gear and Paul Patton in preparing this paper for publication. An earlier version was presented to the Politics of the Body Conference, Performance Space, Sydney, 1987, and was published in *Spectator Burns* 2, 1987.

VICKI KIRBY

8 Corpus delicti: *the body at the scene of writing*

As all of us find ourselves in possession of a body it is not surprising that its ubiquitous matter is the subject of relentless investigation.[1] If our fascination remains undiminished perhaps it is because there is something strangely disconcerting and even alienating in the impossible proximity of this familiar corporeal envelope. Paul Valéry suggests the cause of this uneasy fascination in 'Some Simple Reflections on the Body':

> We speak of [the body] to others as of a thing that belongs to us; but for us it is not entirely a thing; and it belongs to us a little less than we belong to it . . . This thing that is so much mine and yet so mysteriously and sometimes—always, in the end—our most redoubtable antagonist, is the most urgent, the most constant and the most variable thing imaginable: for it carries with it all constancy and all variation.[2]

The enigma of the body is captured then in the troubling question of its location. How are we to identify the fixed transience of this peculiar substance, that 'place' that requires a doubled commentary to capture the ambiguity of 'all constancy and all variation'?

This paradox rehearses a contemporary concern, one that attempts to engage the complexities of any referential gesture. And indeed, the problematic of the body is inseparable from the cognate questions of materiality and/or referentiality. Modernism's crisis of legitimation lies in the faltering recognition that this complicitous kinship of terms can no longer be adjudicated. And as modernism/humanism can be glossed as the discourse of Man, then the hesitations that now interrupt its orthodox accounts of Truth and Subjectivity will inevitably return us to the problematic question of woman.

It would be misleading however to suggest that woman's uncertain identity is only a recent discovery. If second wave feminism were to risk conceiving its own conception, then perhaps its re-birthing would be identified with the emergence of *The Second Sex* in 1949 and the shock of de Beauvoir's curious question 'Are there women really?'.[3] The question is powerful precisely because her argument was able to sustain the scandal of its asking by delaying any easy answer. For, despite all claims to the contrary, there was nothing natural about women according to de Beauvoir. In the now famous opening lines of Book Two, she asserted that 'One is not born, but rather becomes, a woman ... this creature, intermediate between male and eunuch'.[4]

The enigmatic location of woman's specificity has since been interpreted as a symptom of humanism's pervasive narrative, that story line that casts man as the measure of all things. This account positions woman as man's attenuated in-version, as a mere specular reflection through which his identity is grounded. The brute matter of woman's embodiment and the immediacy of her lived experience provide the corporeal substratum upon which man can thereby erect himself and from which he keeps a safe distance. But if the natural world of humanism is denaturalised of its most comfortable wisdoms, then woman's 'place' in this story, her 'in-corporation' into its narrative, becomes undecidable.

Forty years after de Beauvoir, how are we to understand this embodied 'ground' that is 'woman'? Feminists have tirelessly sought to interrogate the meanings of nature and culture in order to broaden woman's horizon of possibilities. And just as de Beauvoir suggested, upon investigation there seems to be nothing very natural about the 'nature of woman'. Consequently, patriarchal attempts to justify woman's subordination as the destined effect of Nature's prescriptions have had to adopt various guises.

Liz Grosz offers a helpful summary of these legitimising strategies in 'A Note on Essentialism and Difference'.[5] She divides these arguments into four kindred, although subtly differentiated, categories: essentialism, biologism, naturalism and universalism. But the terms are easily confused and, as Grosz suggests, each one is often made to serve as a shorthand formula for another. Feminists have become skilled diagnosticians in recognising the conservative commitments invested in this syndrome of justifications and, understandably, a sense of contamination is associated with their pathology. Grosz notes:

> It is not surprising that these terms have become labels for danger zones or theoretical pitfalls in feminist assessments of patriarchal theory ... They are the critical touch-stones of assessment, self-evident guidelines for evaluating patriarchal theories and the patriarchal residues or adherences of feminist theories. These terms seem unquestionably problematic ...[6]

Feminism is usually quick to distance itself from the dubious investments of such terms and to judge the worth of its practice by the success of that distancing. However, Grosz goes on to query the advantage of such an automatic reaction to these categories by cautioning that '. . . their value as criteria of critical evaluation for feminist as well as patriarchal theory is not as clear as they might seem'.[7]

This qualification is pause for thought; an appeal to linger a little longer over feminism's own version of 'doing what comes naturally'. Stepping into the 'danger zone' then, an interesting detail that emerges is that these conservative doxa do not respect the nature/culture divide. It seems that 'the nature of things', or more specifically here, 'the nature of woman', is also discovered in cultural data. For example, Grosz explains that universalism can be conceived in purely social terms, with no necessary recourse to biological arguments. In this case, cross-cultural evidence that shows women consigned to invariant social categories and functions can be offered as proof of essential and therefore unarguable cultural requirements.

The originary cause of what is interpreted as woman's inevitable oppression then is ultimately an arbitrary determination, a theoretical fiction that can variously be secured in both nature and/or culture. Its ambiguous and therefore questionable location is only made stable by patriarchy's own essential investment in the continuing truth of its existence. In other words, man's desire that 'the nature of things'—namely, his privilege—be justified and even demanded by some causal essence in woman, effectively displaces the need for this essential predication from the necessity for his existence to the explanation of hers.

It is surely a partial tribute to the effectiveness of feminism's intellectual persistence and to its tireless re-reading of patriarchal truths that both 'the nature of woman' and indeed, 'nature itself', have still to be reckoned. Given the continued instability of the culture/nature division, maintaining anti-essentialism versus essentialism as the respectively good and bad sides of the argument installs a dubious moral agenda. It also denies feminism's achievements and the mutability of feminism's own identity in negotiating and challenging the different meanings that inform this division in shifting historical contexts. If the field of signification is politically volatile and historically specific, then the continuation of de Beauvoir's enterprise might today be more effectively realised, at least by a certain academic feminism, in a reversal of the apparent direction of its original critique. Refiguring feminism so that it maintains its critical tenacity and relevance, we might now venture a different set of questions. For example, can we remain comfortable with an insistence that there is nothing natural about women? Or more precisely, can we still be sure of just what it is that an affirmative answer to this question defends or denies?

The need to confront such awkward questions was given dramatic expression at a philosophy conference in Canberra. In a paper that argued for the usefulness of Luce Irigaray's work, the speaker rightly assumed that much of her audience would need convincing. Anticipating the charge of essentialism that is commonly levelled at this particular French feminist, a preliminary clarification was offered in her defence. We were told that corporeality in Irigaray's writing was to be understood as a decidedly literary evocation. Those now notorious 'two lips' were a figurative strategy, an attempt to re-read the significance of woman's embodiment as morphology.[8] And finally, to extinguish any lingering doubts that this argument may nevertheless harbour a naturalising impulse, the anatomical or biological body was safely located outside the concerns of Irigaray's interventionist project.

But if most of the audience was reassured by these explanatory remarks, indeed required their expression as a necessary predication before the paper could be taken seriously, I was left wondering just what danger this exclusion had averted. To what *does* the nomination 'biological or anatomical body' refer? Or to put this another way, what secures the separation of its supposed inadmissable meaning from the proper purview of Irigaray's textual interventions?

When I asked a question to this effect it was met with a certain nervous incomprehension. However, deciding that I must still be immersed in a precritical notion of the body, the speaker dismissed me with a revealing theatrical gesture. As if to underline the sheer absurdity of my question, she pinched herself and commented, 'Well, I certainly don't mean *this* body.'

Of course from my particular perspective, the absurdity is not on the side of the question but rather with an answer that insists that a feminist practice can effectively engage the problematic of corporeality *without* meaning this body. Just where then is that 'other' body to be located? And how is it so quickly and decidedly dissociated from the flesh of this one? What this anecdote illustrates is the pervasive belief that the anatomical body is indeed the unarguably real body, the literal body, the body whose immovable and immobilising substance must be secured outside the discussion. This improper body is quarantined for fear that its ineluctable immediacy will leave us no space for change, no chance to be other-wise, no place from which to engender a different future. According to this view, the politics of representation remain separable from what are commonly understood as the biological facts of the body's existence. And inevitably, the sex/gender, real/representation distinction will reassert its comfortable wisdom precisely because it reiterates the most adequate conceptualisation of materiality as something fundamentally other than its interpretation.[9]

However the powerful attraction of recent developments in Continental philosophy has included the disruption of this base/ superstructure model as well as the promise of suggestive possibilities for re-reading the question of *how* reality means. Feminism has actively participated in this radical enterprise. And yet even in feminisims that are informed and empowered by this same critique of a restricted notion of materiality, an accompanying manoeuvre can 'naturally' exclude the biological body from critical attention. If pinching oneself is indeed a reality test, albeit within the ironised quotation marks of a certain theoretical savvy, then announcing that reality's substance is of no matter suggests an unshakeable belief that it matters too much. Although it is an unconscious lamentation of the fact, this announcement nevertheless unwittingly evidences a profound faith in patriarchy's foundational truths. It witnesses an unquestioning devotion that refigures patriarchy's terms through a negative theology. What we have located here is what is believed to be essentialism's superlative; what is most essential, most incontrovertibly real and most decidedly significant. For we admit that reality's harshest truth is the anatomical body when we determine to disavow its effect/substance by simply dissolving the accompanying notions of 'reality' and 'reference' through which it is made manifest.

However over the last few years there have been hesitant yet increasing signs that 'essentialism', as it is commonly understood, is not necessarily 'something' from which we could, or should, dissociate ourselves.[10] Nor is this view bought at the expense of recognising the violence that is essentialism. For example, in the aformentioned article by Liz Grosz, she acknowledges: 'Any theory of femininity, any definition of woman in general, any description that abstracts from the particular, historical, cultural, ethnic and class positions of women verges perilously close to essentialism'.[11] Grosz goes on to cite Toril Moi, who also asserts that '. . . to define 'woman' is necessarily to essentialize her'. But Grosz is alert to an attendant irony in this assertion to which Moi remains blind. Moi's description of essentialism, especially when she describes it as the defining attribute of Luce Irigaray's work, represents an unequivocal judgement against such definitions, a condemnation of their fixed investments, a casting out of their error. For Moi rightly understands that, 'any attempt to formulate a general theory of femininity will be metaphysical'.[12] Moi witnesses something unholy in Irigaray's work, and censures her for '. . . fall[ing] for the temptation to produce her own positive theory of femininity'.[13] Grosz uncovers the paradox that this belief enacts:

> ... if women cannot be characterised in any general way ... then how can feminism be taken seriously? What justifies the assumption that women are oppressed as a sex? What, indeed, does it mean to talk about women as a category? If we are not justified in taking women as a category, then what political grounding does feminism have?[14]

Moi's fervid desire to remain unsullied by essentialism forgets that essentialism is the condition of possibility for any political axiology: the minimal consensual stuff that political action fastens onto is already essentialism's effect. There is no 'outside' this entanglement. However, the task is not to dream of deliverance, of yet another theology that promises to transcend this contamination. Rather, it is to begin to real-ise that we are inextricably immersed within that contamination and that our fundamental complicity with it is, strangely, its enabling moment.

For example, if we return to de Beauvoir's defiant question, 'Are there women really?', both Toril Moi and the speaker in my anecdote would seem to answer its challenge with a definite no. But such an answer, indeed any definitive answer, misunderstands the political purchase that the question commands precisely because it sustains an interrogative force *within* what we now call phallocentrism. That is to say, the 'other' of phallocentrism resides within its house, albeit in an uncanny location.

Re-thinking essentialism, then, is not a dispute about its meaning, at least not within the order of its commonplace understanding. The weight of that understanding as the burden of its lived reality is not in contention here. If anything, what is being questioned is how we can pretend to bear this burden so lightly. It is not so much the meaning of essentialism that requires further consideration, but 'the how' of that meaning. How is 'essence' entailed, made proper, installed 'as such' and naturalised within our thought and our being? How does it congeal into an embodied reality? If we assume that when we locate essentialism we identify it and corral its dangers the better to determine the virtue of our own practice, we have merely embraced another of essentialism's many mutations and one that finds us right inside the belly of the beast.[15]

Essentialism is not an entity that can be identified and dissolved by saying yes or no to it. For example, when Toril Moi says no to the category 'woman', to '... the minefield of femininity and femaleness'[16] she imagines herself a witness to the truth of (the) matter, or more precisely, to truth's essence (assuming that there could be such a thing)—to the non-truth of phallocentrism's truth—namely, to the truth of its error. But even if we were to grant that essentialism is unarguably wrong—morally, politically and logically—then we still haven't addressed the ways in which its 'errors' work; how essentialism's scriptures 'come to matter', how they come to write/right themselves.

To put this in a way that better suggests that we are always/already in the grip of essentialism's reflex, we could ask 'Where is the evidence for either essentialism's error or anti-essentialism's truth to be situated and of what does it consist?' Or, 'Against what criteria or with what 'matter' is the category 'woman' considered incommensurable?'

The 'place' from which both essentialism and anti-essentialism make their claims is 'something' of a 'share accommodation', a strange abode in which their contradictions co-habit. And this abode recalls a body that demonstrates its anti-essentialism by pinching its essentialism, a body that denies the violence of identity on the one hand by violently grasping its identity with the other.

Essentialism has always been of interest to feminism but only recently has this interest been thought to pay dividends. Emerging discussions of essentialism are attempting to confront feminism's anxieties the better to exorcise the somatophobia that underpins the legacy of phallocentrism's mind/body split. But the issue still conjures fear as well as fascination, even, or perhaps especially, among critical theorists. In a recent article, Diana Fuss suggests that: 'Perhaps more than any other notion in the vocabulary of recent feminist poststructuralist theory, 'essentialism' has come to represent both our greatest fear and our greatest temptation . . . essentialism is the issue which simply refuses to die.'[17] Accordingly, the subject is commonly approached with a certain sense of hesitation and guilt. Fuss notes the apologetic tone that accompanies the question's reconsideration, with critics consistently describing their enterprise as one of 'risking' or 'daring' to consider essentialism's revaluation.

And yet although rethinking essentialism marks an avowed return to the body, it is not an easy homecoming. Indeed the reunion is always be-ing deferred. Perhaps commerce with the body is risky business because the border between the mind/body split, the border across which interpretations of the body might be negotiated, just cannot be secured. This fear of being unwittingly discovered behind enemy lines, caught in the suffocating and powerful embrace of that carnal envelope, menaces all conciliatory efforts. Feminism needs courage to mount even quite small and furtive reconnaissance missions across that border. And any exchange between the mind and the body will demand explanation, a minimal reassurance that incursions into the body's foreign spaces will be temporary and provisional, a 'tactical' or 'strategic' necessity that justifies the risks. Through all of this, it would seem that the body is still figured as a dangerous and hostile territory that demands a cautious itinerary if it is to be approached at all.

The body of Luce Irigaray's work has become a synecdoche for these larger threats.[18] To involve oneself in her 'writing (of) the body' is a venture that has come to require justification. And these justifications will routinely stress Irigaray's theoretical and philosophical sophistication and the ways in which the pleasures of her text are enabled by the crisis of confidence in orthodox understandings of referentiality and materiality. The question, however, is what to do with what Jane Gallop describes as Irigaray's supposed 'referential naïveté'; the seduction that Irigaray enacts by way of a thinking through of anatomical reference. The speaker in my earlier anecdote was determined to solve this apparent problem by discarding anatomy as something outside the play of textual intervention. As a result, it will be recalled that Irigaray's 'two lips' were considered to be a form of figuration and not a literalisation.

Jane Gallop is of a different persuasion. In 'Quand Nos Lèvres S'Écrivent: Irigaray's Body Politic', she argues that anatomy is inextricably caught up in its interpretation: 'Discourse about the body seems to represent a point of unusually suggestive tension about the referent. Yet perhaps the most far-reaching effect of her (Irigaray's) *invraisemblable* stand on the labia is to force the reader to reconsider the status of anatomical referentiality.'[19] Gallop goes on to conclude that 'the gesture of a troubled but nonetheless insistent referentiality is essential.'[20] And she defends this opinion by way of a slippery rhetorical gambit that demonstrates that the referent is a necessary anchor for any argument, even as it remains elusive and ambiguous.

Gallop opens her manoeuvre by remembering Freud's famous dictum, 'anatomy is destiny'. She notes that Irigaray 'seems' to endorse what she describes as Freud's folly in this assumption, but advises, 'let us beware too literal a reading of Irigarayan anatomy'.[21] Gallop answers this too literal reading by reminding us that Irigaray's object is not genital anatomy but the symbolic interpretation of that anatomy, the ways in which a phallomorphic logic reconstructs anatomy in its own image. But having put this corrective into place, Gallop openly admits that her argument entails some sticky dealings with an extra-textual referent, a male anatomy that, somehow, informs phallomorphism. It seems then that although the body is an interpretation, the power of its interpretations induces an '*effet de réel*', or 'referential illusion' as Gallop describes it.[22] It is an illusion, it would seem, that insists as anatomy.

Hence, for Gallop, all realities are mediated by textuality. 'Belief in simple referentiality . . . cannot recognise that the reality to which it appeals is a traditional ideological construction . . . [T]raditional idealogical constructs which are not recognised as such ... are taken for the "real"'.[23] An illustration of this misrecognition might be feminism's own participation in the either/or sexology of vagina or clitoris. Gallop discovers in this debate an unwitting commitment to a phallologic whose sense of choice (between clitoris as phallus-same, or vagina as phallus-opposite) is, consequently, quite mistaken. According to Gallop, Irigaray's genius is that she is not similarly duped: 'Irigaray seems to be advocating a female sexuality that replaces the anxious either-or with a pleasurable both: vagina *and* clitoris. But Irigaray ultimately chooses *not both but neither*, and the spark of her genital poetics rather comes to light on the lips.'[24] As Gallop would have it, the empirical appeal of clitoris and/or vagina is rejected because: 'Irigaray is interested in a plurality that is not reducible to a series of singular elements. In the list of female genital parts, only the lips are already plural'.[25]

However, Gallop's reading of the body in/of Irigaray's writing is itself a dissection of female genital parts, a selection from a series of singular (even when plural) elements. For Gallop secures the valued plurality of 'the two lips' only by an excision that removes the contamination of both vagina and clitoris. It seems that Gallop's notion of plurality is a strangely restricted one, and one that is bought at considerable expense. But Gallop, of course, can afford to pay the price that these circumcisions incur because, after all, 'the place' that is be-ing re-formed is a textual site, a plastic space that is remade through the clever surgery that writing performs. Hence, according to this view, there is 'really' no price to be paid, because this reinterpretation negotiates an '*effet de réel*', a '*poétique du corps*' that recreates embodiment and re-views the status normally accorded to an immutable, anatomical referentiality.

If we translate this re-formation into the familiar terms of the nature/culture, essentialism/anti-essentialism division, then it appears that Gallop dissipates a certain anxiety about what to do with anatomy (nature, essence) by arguing that anatomy is always/already just another moment in culture's refiguring of itself. In other words, anatomy is an illusion of sorts, albeit a very powerful one, and one that Gallop imbues with a certain political efficacy. Understandably, it is this belief in anatomy's political efficacy that motivates its reinterpretation. According to Gallop, the body 'as such', its 'essential matter', is always/already deferred because of 'the absence of any certain access to the referent'.[26] It follows from this that the anxieties that accompanied the mind/body border crossing were largely unfounded. There was no enemy waiting in ambush. Indeed, in essence, it seems that there was no-body there at all.

But what about biology? Does Gallop's interpretation of Irigaray's virtuoso re-writing (of) the body include in its textual adventure the peristaltic movements of the viscera, the mitosis of cells, the electrical activity that plays across a synapse, the itinerary of a virus etc.? In other words, is this a 'text' and a 'writing' that includes all the oozings and pulsings that literally and figuratively make up the stuff of the body's extra-ordinary circuitry? Apparently not. (Certainly Gallop is careful never to say as much.)[27]

Returning to the problematic of essentialism/corporeality, it seems that I must now take my turn and dare to ask, again, 'But why not?' Is this perhaps because within such an inquiry all the brave rhetoric of our risk taking finally threatens to deliver up the full reality of its promise? And just what is the full reality of this promise?

It should be said up front that Gallop's interpretation of Irigaray is a welcome relief from the sober, flat-footed and largely uninformed commentaries that so often advise against the complexities of her work.[28] Gallop's writing scintillates. It playfully and provocatively explores the resonances between female sexuality and modernist textuality in Irigaray's corporeal *poiésis* and its value is not in dispute here. Rather, my argument concerns the way that Gallop, along with other of Irigaray's more subtle and careful interpreters, have underestimated the force of both Irigaray's writing and indeed of their own.

Gallop acknowledges the confounded nature of any argument that claims to separate the supposed brute matter of anatomy from its interpretation. Nevertheless, the force of Gallop's corrective against those who would confuse Irigaray's '*effet de réel*' with 'the real', or conflate 'referential illusion' with 'referential naïveté', is predicated on the necessity for just such a separation. Gallop is able to resolve this contradiction because she reads 'anatomy' in a restricted sense, as the body's surface—the forms that are to be re-formed, the text that is to be re-inscribed. Consequently, morphology is accorded its narrowest interpretation as the metaphorisation of sexual difference; the unity of phallomorphism; the split-that-is-not-one of vulvomorphism. Within this interpretation, Irigaray's writing traces its artistry over the surface of the body as writing pad, beating a tattoo that suggests different patterns through which its meanings may be ciphered. Gallop offers a concise annotation to the inflection that motivates this performance, 'Irigarayan *poétique du corps* is not an expression of the body but a *poiésis*, a creating of the body.'[29] But how does Gallop determine the difference between 'a creating of the body' and 'an expression of the body', and why is this division necessary?

Gallop appears to conceive writing, or *poéisis*, through its phenomenal analogue—as an activity whose effects are passively received and recorded upon a surface. However, in other arenas feminism is wise to the dubious sexual economy that informs this notion of writing. The model of a *tabula rasa*, whose inert matter merely receives and then bears an inscription without in any way re-writing its significance, is surely familiar. The body/woman, as that specular surface, is routinely denied any efficacy in the reproduction of value.

Gallop's hermeneutic 'secludes' biology behind anatomy's dermal veil. Perhaps the referent is also hidden behind that veil, deep within the body's inaccessible depths. It will be remembered that Gallop describes the complexities of the referent in terms of accessibility. And this closure that installs an inaccessible 'before' or 'behind', is consistent with Gallop's reliance on a psychoanalytic narrative that traditionally posits the body before language. Psychoanalysis does not engage the body as itself a field of language but rather as something which precedes and then enters the field of language.[30] Gallop also draws on literary theory which has tended to read the notion of 'textuality', or 'writing', back into the confines of a convenient hermeneutic horizon, as if to preserve and contain 'context' within the covers of a book.[31] One has only to note the consistency with which literary critics continue to conflate Derrida's notion of 'writing in the general sense' with writing in the phenomenal sense, to appreciate what is at stake in maintaining this crude reading.[32]

Rethinking essentialism is a thinking through the body, and this is the thinking through of closure; essentialism's identifying gesture. But how do we think this 'corporeal place', this envelope of immanence that our disembodied speculations would render 'separable' and 'other'? Again we are reminded of a body that pinches itself within the reflex of a möbius loop. Enacting the circuit of a contradiction, anatomy grasps its own excess, the neither/nor of essentialism and anti-essentialism that nevertheless, and at once, embraces them both; the literal and figural tissue of their mutual implication.

Biology's scriptures cannot be left out of this account. Biology is volatile; a mutable intertexture—a discursive effect. It is the stuff that informs our interventions. And such is the implication of biology that Irigaray's '*poétique du corps*' might also be thought as biology rewriting itself. The involution of such a circuit conjures Derrida's discussion of the writing-machine in Freud's 'neurological fable'—the mystic writing pad.[33] And if we think the body as the scene of writing/reading, then propriation is indeterminate. In other words, we can never settle on a causal beginning. 'Writing' is inflected through a sexual diacritics, what Sarah Kofman has called, 'a sexualization of the text' and 'a textualization of sex'.[34] 'Woman' is held in place, indeed becomes the place, that must inherit the burden of a difference that is no difference; phallogocentrism's 'logic of the same'.

However, as 'woman' is ceaselessly re-figured as an absence in every account, such that Man can be rendered present, the very repetition of this mode of reckoning exceeds the 'logic of the same'. 'Woman' is the embodied place in which essentialism comes to reside, albeit uncannily. Essentialism is transformational: it is never identical with itself. Consequently, 'woman' embodies the 'play' of essentialism's difference from and within itself in the mode of production of Man. This 'play' that accompanies the exchange of value can also be described as 'work', because it engenders material effects: the production of inscription.[35]

'Woman' is the embodiment of phallocentrism's infinite essentialisms, the tissue of their complicitous interlacings. 'Woman' is the manifestation, the 'reality', that 'references' essentialism's constitutive violations. And her body is indeed essentialism's superlative precisely because it matters *too* much, because it wears too many meanings, too many contradictions, too many questions that defy resolution and that stay alive in the paradoxical spacing of their peculiar assemblage. Within the space of this inter-texture and contexture, between and within the interstices of essentialism's textile, a persistent and radical singularity insists. And this singularity or radical difference always remains essentialism's accomplice: the 'constant variable' that allows essentialism to play the imposture of 'invariant constancy'. This spacing 'is' the impossible complexity that women really are and whose morphology women embody.

Morphology then is not anatomy, or indeed biology, although it must nevertheless include them.[36] We might think morphology as 'the how' of the valorisation of value.[37] If we return to the question of the referent as it pertains to woman's embodiment, and think it as morphology, then Gallop's earlier discussion of its accessibility remains inadequate to this complexity. The referent isn't so much hidden, or out of reach behind the adumbration of an '*effet de réel*'. Rather, the referent is an immanence, a semiological complicity or binding together of traces. And the complexity of this weaving is such that the referent never quite coincides with itself. Not so much a veiling then as a partitioning—an intricate and infinite fabric-ation.[38]

Perhaps I can finish where I began, that is, with de Beauvoir's question, 'Are there women really?' I have argued that a feminist practice cannot afford to say either yes or no to this question any more than it can afford to embrace the impasse. However, we can attend to 'the how' of 'becoming woman' as that process by which the answer's undecidability is determined. The political purchase in the question, 'What is woman really' is embodied in 'the grammatical mark of identity'—the copula 'is'.[39] For 'woman' is never identical with herself—the copula is always/already a supplement. However, the process of woman's becoming is not the counter-narrative of the decentred subject doing battle with phallocentrism's centred subject.

'Woman', the subject of morphology, is not cognisable. Morphology cannot be secured as a way that women 'with theory' might practice their own peculiar form of consciousness raising.[40]

De Beauvoir's 'woman question' then has political efficacy because it broaches the possibility that Man could be the object of this question. And Gayatri Spivak, attending to this possibility, and acknowledging that the economy of sexual difference is a complicitous one, asks, 'What is man that the itinerary of his desire creates such a text?'[41]

'Becoming woman' is written in the space of inscription, and we might name that spacing with the non-name *différance*.[42] However, 'woman' should not be thought *as* the non-name *différance*. Lacking propriety, the two may appear the same. And indeed, Derrida has used 'woman' as a name for *différance*, acknowledging the paleonymic burden of the word's undecidability.[43]

Nevertheless, *différance* is better understood as the condition of possibility, the spacing, in which woman's embodiment is inscribed. This isn't a reversible notion. *Différance* should be thought as an exceeding that is, again, in excess of 'the excess that is woman'. In other words, when we insist that the copula is not *adequate* to represent woman's be-ing, let us not turn this into a nonsense whereby woman is denied an embodied existence. We are surely attempting instead to acknowledge something of the complex process through which this existence is formed.

Related to this point, Gayatri Spivak has made a valuable intervention against feminism's desire to read 'woman' as the privileged space of a general alterity that is coincident under the catachresis *différance*. Spivak encourages us to think the difference within the spacing of *différance*. 'Let us divide the name of woman so that we see ourselves as naming, not merely named', and with all due caution to the violence of turning a name into a simple referent, she suggests: 'Today, here, what I call the 'gendered subaltern', especially in decolonised space, has become the name "woman" for me.'[44]

I have also come to think the disenfranchised subaltern subject as the other of woman.[45] However, I prefer to mark that difference, an unimaginable difference, with the catachrestical name *différance*. I am not convinced that the name 'woman' can be thought of as just a name, a catachresis without a literal referent. I have tried to argue that this name, albeit a wrong name, is never immaterial. For if women matter at all, it is as this word's embodied realisation.

PART IV
And Spaces

STEVEN RUGARE

9 The advent of America at EPCOT Center

EPCOT Center, the permanent world's fair at Florida's Disney World, stands as a late moment in the history of world's fairs, and there has perhaps been no tourist better equipped to introduce us to that tradition, and hence to EPCOT Center itself, than America's great eccentric historiographer/autobiographer, Henry Adams. In *The Education of Henry Adams*, he writes of himself, 'He professed the religion of World's Fairs, without which he held education to be a blind impossibility.'[1] And this religion of his was a religion of ethical geometry, of spatialising metaphors, of a triangulation by which Adams hoped to locate his own tenuous authority somewhere between the two great shrines which he compares in his text, namely the great churches with which the France of the twelfth and thirteenth centuries dedicated itself to the singular good taste and grace of the Virgin, and the world's fairs with which the West of the nineteenth and twentieth centuries has attempted to exhibit to itself the totality of its achievement and the full scope of its project.

And it is above all the possibility of complete vision that draws Adams to worship at the Great Exhibition of 1900 and the numerous other great fairs of his age. In the displays of the age's technological achievements, in the plenitude of products which makes for a fair, he discerns the spatial articulation of an occult historical narrative. And this narrative, as is proper for a pilgrim's progress, has an ecstatic and eschatological component. What the fair maps out is what Adams also found in his studies of the orbits of comets, the ever-accelerating approach of the moment of perihelion, the climactic epiphany when the sun is as close as can be. Beyond that moment, thought Adams, the liturgy of historical forces had to circle around to the advent of something utterly new. Speaking of the Saint Louis Exposition of 1904, he says:

> One asked oneself whether this extravagance reflected the past or imagined the future; whether it was a creation of the old American or a promise of the new one. No prophet could be believed, but a pilgrim of power . . . might allow himself to hope. The prospect from the Exposition was pleasant: one seemed to see almost an adequate motive for power; almost a scheme for progress.[2]

Of course, Adams' pilgrim's optimism is only a momentary transport. Instead of revealing the path to progress, his pilgrimage reveals that the Exposition is nothing other than a mechanism for discerning connections between disparate items, a place for framing world views, for including all nations and objects in a global perspective, no matter how trivial or incommensurate they may normally seem to be.

Precisely because the exposition always gives a semblance of revelation, or even a promise of absolution, because it attempts to remember the World (as inhabited by historical Man) past, present *and* future, it can also be seen as an attempt to perform the entire historical drama *now*, while there's *still time*—to go for a last canonical moment of apocalyptic disclosure before the whole project of the World collapses into decay or destruction or sheer incomprehensibility. This is what Umberto Eco suggests in his essay 'A Theory of Expositions'.

> At first contact and first reaction, exhibitions assume the form of an inventory, an immense catalogue of things produced by man in all countries over the past ten thousand years, displayed so that humanity will not forget them. They seem to be a final recapitulation in the face of a hypothetical end of the world.[3]

In attempting to get one's bearings at EPCOT Center, it's important to bear this tradition of world's expositions in mind. EPCOT has similar ambitions to many of its predecessors. Like most great world's fairs it affects the comprehensive and absolutely present spectacle of the world, all carefully ordered and available for visual consumption. Like most expositions, it also functions in a particular relation to its primary audience, Americans, and serves to place America in relation to the world, in much the same way that, for example, Brisbane's World Expo 88 was an act of national and civic boosterism.

What is lacking at EPCOT is the sheer plenitude of objects, the real souvenirs of human activity that are inventoried in the traditional world's fair. To the extent that the contents of 'culture' or 'technology' are required at EPCOT Center, they are simulated, but not primarily with the intent of exhibiting the actual objects.[4] At

EPCOT, the clutter and plenitude of the traditional world's fair has been discreetly managed into something very different. This is named by Eco when, a few pages after the definition quoted above, he discusses the way meaning works in the architecture of the exposition. 'In an exposition we show not the objects but the exposition itself.'[5] In EPCOT, this essential proposition is disengaged from the curio cabinet of 'objects', and the exposition, instead of gathering itself together in anticipation of apocalypse, becomes itself purely apocalyptic. The end of the world is no longer the exposition's hypothesis; it is its *a priori.* EPCOT gives to spectation an architectonic diagram of the world, a revelation of the semiotic and symbolic contracts by which the world has been made viewable, knowable, and useful and by which American identity can be placed in, or perhaps subsequent to, the world.

With these ideas in mind, I will now give a brief tour of EPCOT Center. EPCOT is, as the guide book informs us, 'really two unique worlds in one',[6] and indeed EPCOT is composed of two interlocking rings of exhibits, each of which functions according to its own means of exposition. The first 'world' the visitor encounters is Future World, which consists of a ring of self-contained pavilions, each of which portrays some aspect of the technological future as realised by the architects and 'imagineers' of WED (Walter Elias Disney) Enterprises in cooperation with a major corporate sponsor. These buildings are 'accessed' through an architecturally neutral central space called the 'Communicore'. Future World is announced (along with all of EPCOT) by a huge spherical structure called 'Spaceship Earth' and is traversed by the Disney World Monorail, which connects EPCOT to the Magic Kingdom (the Florida version of the California Disneyland) and the other components of the Disney World complex.[7]

There is no multiplicity of cultures in Future World, which is another way of saying that the technological future is presented as America's future. Cultural difference is the business of the other 'world' of EPCOT, the World Showcase, which is framed by Future World. World Showcase exposes the multiplicity of the Future's heritage by disposing a series of structures representing various foreign countries around the shores of the neutral expanse of a lagoon. These exhibits do not take the form of national pavilions but of scaled down townscapes similar in type to the Mainstreet USA[8] by which one enters the Magic Kingdom and the California Disneyland. These little collages are not understood, as would be the pavilions at a traditional world's fair, to be representative of the achievements of the nations that sent them. Rather, in EPCOT semantics, they simply *are* the nations as wholes. Thus, the World Showcase Lagoon is not ringed by pavilions *from* Mexico, Norway or China. It is ringed by Mexico, Norway and China themselves.

In its basic functioning World Showcase reproduces many of the characteristics of the suburban environment that is proliferating through central Florida, somewhere beyond the boundaries of the Disney domain. It is an outdoor space in which a surprising array of styles, forms and symbols are juxtaposed in such a way that difference is represented as plurality, or as the presence of identity. Each country is composed of small-scale representations of its characteristic, traditional architecture. In some cases, these buildings are recognisable, iconic structures. For example, 'Italy' reproduces in fairly careful detail just enough of the Piazza San Marco (the Doge's Palace and the campanile) to place us in Venice.[9]

Looking into the little streets of the various 'countries', one sees the effort to break up walls and surfaces, to allow the boundaries of the street to expand and contract, so as to give the effect of an interrelated, accidental, unplanned, organic, humane urban space. This kind of false streetscape was developed by the Disney architects and has since become a prime tenet of shopping mall design, as well as a favourite technique of postmodern architects.[10]

The effects of this sort of space can hardly be underestimated. In these purposely irregular, organic spaces, the private and potentially liberatory experience of ambling through the city is rendered predictable and profitable. Michel de Certeau has discussed the narrativity of walking through the modern orthogonally planned city as a kind of resistant rhetoric, an improvisatory and embodied troping that cannot help but get something back from the rational planners and the police. But here at Disney World, under the banner of a kind of humanism, under the terms of 'user-friendly' space, the spatial practices de Certeau describes are seemingly anticipated, and their traces are accounted for in the built environment.[11]

In fact, there is rather little to do in World Showcase except consume the narrative provided by this ripe space, this space the essence of which wants to be (in Benjamin's words) 'consummated in distraction'. It is the presence of the country as generated by the architecture which justifies the experience of eating its food, seeing its traditional dances, and buying its mass-produced souvenirs. In other words, the EPCOT world's fair replicates the visual experience of tourism and obviates the necessity of visiting the actual place. Moreover, since the EPCOT architecture shows only what is most characteristic, traditional, and typical about the places it simulates, it improves upon real foreign cities, in which 'historic' architecture is likely to be unpleasantly juxtaposed with modern buildings in the international style. Such a contamination would imply, for the tourist, a confusion of the expected patterns of commerce between tradition and progress, between familiar and foreign, and might ultimately result in some question about the validity and effects of the tourist's quest to consume foreign places and peoples. So, EPCOT draws a line between the singularity of the Future and the multiplicity of 'cultures', keeping each from a contamination that might distort the truth it reveals. The World Showcase is appropriately named in that it exposes the world as a display of objects ready for appropriation, all foreign and different but all equally easily consumed.

The visual mediation of plurality is reinforced by the flat expanse of the lagoon, which unifies the entire composition by giving views of a skyline combining castles, pagodas, temples and palaces of various nationalities, so that, looking out from any one country, the visitor sees a panorama of all the others, a clear view of the variety of the world. This panoptic display is the almost literal achievement of the showcase metaphor, and a great deal of trouble has been taken in the composition of these vistas. For example, the Eiffel Tower is included to be seen from across the lake, though it cannot be approached from France at all.

These juxtapositions of disparate signs are both jarring and amusing, but their effect is, I think, the concentration of meaning, rather than its dispersion. The architectural collage of the showcase, the collection of presences signified around the lagoon, figures the presence of the world (and of Man) as a collection of distinct yet essentially similar units.[12]

There is one exception, one violation of the boundary between the Showcase and Future World: the building/place/narrative called The American Adventure. Since, unlike the other countries, America cannot be or does not need to be made present as a totality, it is given a qualifying title and a qualifying temporality. Instead of representing 'America' outside any particulars of history, The American Adventure is an explicit memorial of America's founding, and this advent is remembered 'through a magical mix of motion pictures and *Audio-Animatronics* "imagineering" hosted by Ben Franklin and Mark Twain'. The building is, of course, in the 'colonial' style by which, because of its reference to the founding, oblivion is figured as history in so many suburban houses. The adventure is treated as a single building, not a townscape, and consists entirely of an auditorium and a waiting area decorated with quotes from an odd collection of ostensibly famous Americans.

The show plays fairly loosely with historical facts, but turns out to be more complex than one would expect. The optimistic Ben Franklin is played off against the more skeptical Mark Twain, and the whole presents an ambivalent narrative. A suitably inspirational conclusion is achieved only by the most overt means—a booming choral soundtrack and, quite strikingly, the cessation of all attempts at explanation or narration of history since World War II, after which point events are allowed to play themselves out as montage. Instead of a singular narrative closure, there is the repetition of a seemingly disjointed series of iconic images from 'news', television and films, a plurality that cannot be encompassed in a single view, and does not have to be. No-one expects there to be a syntactical connection between Vietnam, Elvis and Liz Taylor, but they make present an identity (albeit diachronically) just as effectively as do the architectures disposed around the World Showcase Lagoon. A totalising effect is achieved without ever explicitly bringing a totality into view.

This is ultimately quite effective, as the images are familiar and powerful, but it combines uncomfortably with the kind of narrative of the unfolding of the American 'spirit' that seems to be intended. This tension is displayed most notably by the presence of a series of statues of the 'Spirits of America,' placed in niches on the side walls of the auditorium. These white, ghostly figures, representing various American qualities (a farmer for 'self-reliance', a cowboy for 'individualism', Puritans for 'religion', a sea captain out of Winslow Homer for 'adventure') serve the kind of stereotyped narrative closure, a plurality bound together by sentiment, that one expects from Disney, and, sure enough, they are garishly backlit, one after another, during the closing chords of the show. Coming so soon after the much slipperier montage of post-war America, these overly explicit plaster ghosts represent, and fairly risibly, a certain failure to recover narrative for propagandistic purposes. This sense of failure is only intensified by the emotional force of the images in the montage, and the show's concluding gesture towards exaltation—with hosts Franklin and Twain 'live' on stage, surveying the future from the walkway on the torch of the Statue of Liberty while the music swells beneath them—generates a response less from a sense of fulfilled narrative purpose than from sheer excess.

As opposed to the carefully deployed variety of World Showcase, Future World aims for a sort of utopian unity. Instead of giving a unified presentation of different places with different styles, of a multiplicity of pasts made absolutely present, Future World is to be understood as one place, as an orderly array of the different aspects of a singular future. The exposition of these aspects is primarily accomplished by a series of multimedia narrative set-ups, in which the visitor is conveyed to the future by way of an 'historical' narrative told by a complex series of projected images and audio-animatronic dioramas.

While World Showcase consists primarily of exterior space, almost all of the action of Future World is indoors, and the pavilions are, like The American Adventure, to be read as single buildings. For the most part, their interiors are not architectural space at all, not space in which people appear to one another. They are instead fragmented, unfathomable spaces, through which people are disposed toward the always-present spectacle of the world. The buildings are largely taken up by the exhibit machinery and by the ancillary spaces that manage the queues waiting to see the exhibits. This tendency to fragment movement and compartmentalise perception contrasts strikingly with the subtlety and skill with which World Showcase makes way for an apparently free and organic experience. The pavilions of Future World are thus highly ordered machines of presence, in which EPCOT Center's guests are as carefully deployed as all the story-telling gadgetry through which they are run.

The content of these stories is not too surprising. The Exxon 'Universe of Energy' pavilion discusses the importance of protecting the environment while still assuring us that 'safe, reliable' nuclear energy has a place in our future. It tells us about the importance of developing solar energy, but neglects to tell us that Exxon recently sold its solar energy subsidiary. Meanwhile, at 'The Living Seas', United Technologies is also talking about the fragility of the eco-system, while simultaneously informing us that there are enormous resources in the sea, just waiting for us to build undersea cities and exploit them. At 'The Land' Kraft wants us to know how much it values the small family farm, the disappearance of which is blamed on naturalised 'market forces', among which Kraft does not, of course, count itself.

For the moment, it would serve little purpose to make too much of these often incoherent tales. They are, of course, chock full of shocking lies, and they could lead to some rather pertinent questions, like who or what *is* United Technologies? And there are certainly real stakes in such questions and in the machinery that occasions them. After all, United Technologies (like each of its sibling corporations) paid $300 million for a ten-year lease on the rights to 'present' its pavilion,[13] which suggests that they think that Disney can insure a substantial ideological return on their narrative investments.

I am inclined to wonder what they get for their money, to wonder if the 'imagineers' at Disney and its sponsors really get what it means to experience their gadgetry. Because Future World so fully deploys its monologic story of the technological future, I've come to think that it may produce certain residual narrative possibilities that cannot be built into the process in the same way that they are built into the apparently more open and available space of the World Showcase.

In part, the residual value of Future World derives from the disturbing tiredness of the Future. While the present changes a great deal, nothing ever changes in the Future except the date when the Future will take place. Thus, the Future that is now projected for 'sometime in the next century' is, for all practical purposes, the Future that was projected with much the same Disney technology at the 1964 World's Fair, except *that* future should have happened by now.

This point is all but acknowledged in the Horizons pavilion, presented by General Electric. Since Horizons purports to be a comprehensive portrayal of life in the future, the narrative evidence for the truth of what it displays is given by way of a brief history of projected 'futures', beginning with Jules Verne and working its way up to the 1950s, approximately to the aesthetic of *The Jetsons*. The point of this story is to show the way in which the future has been projected within the aesthetic and technological horizons (pun not intended) of those who projected it. Having made this perfectly sensible point, the narrative voice of the journey then proclaims that the Horizons of the present cannot be doubted on the same grounds because they are based on soundly 'scientific' predictions (as if all the previous futures weren't). We are then shown the same future that has been revolving around the Carousel of Progress since 1964 or before. A family, dispersed across all zones of the earth and orbital space, is brought together by modern communications technology so that everyone can participate in a child's birthday,[14] and (despite minor updatings of gender and racial politics) this is still that same old family of tomorrow, living in the same paradise of colonies in space, cities under the sea, farms in the deserts, videophones, and household robots.

It might be accurate to say that the future of Future World is, in fact, past. Stylistically, nothing in Future World dates much past the early 1970s. This is particularly obvious in the exterior architectures of the pavilions, which come in an ever-so-slightly discordant range of modernisms and which make no architectural attempts to acknowledge each other. While some of the pavilions have the sleek, reflective look of Silicon Valley, others look expressionistic, and still others have the sort of white, clean, space-age look familiar from films such as *2001*.[15]

At the level of graphic consumption, the future of Future World tends to become plural. This is highly significant, since, as is generally the case with non-text-based presentations, the primary activity of Future World is not the consumption of information, but the consumption of imagery *and* the simultaneous consumption of the clever gadgetry that produces the imagery. This interpretation allows us to consider the receivers of EPCOT as something other than the bovine creatures of false-consciousness that a number of writers on the subject have postulated.[16] It becomes possible to construe the consumption of EPCOT as an active process, in which is deployed a basic competency in the consumption of both the techniques of mediation by which EPCOT's 'worlds' are produced and the stylistic and symbolic codes out of which they are constructed.[17] EPCOT is as much an event of recognition as it is an event of revelation. Seen in these terms, the slight variations in graphic style between the various world-devices of Future World and the resultant multiplication of the futures they narrate disclose a portrait of a world in which differentiation always seeps out of too-close identification, the replication of the future leads to a dispersal of presence, and the gadgetry that forms the possibility of simulation itself acquires a certain onto-theological standing.

This view is substantially confirmed by the design of the connective elements of Future World. Unlike the World Showcase Lagoon, which gives simultaneous visual access to the entire world, the 'Communicore' seems to be designed as a visual and kinetic barrier between the incipient future worldlets of Future World. It is an interstitial, neutral space designed to look like it could be anywhere, and its atopy mediates visual connections between the various pavilions by both architectural and—given its dedication to 'networking' and informatics—narrative means.

What is visible throughout Future World and throughout most of EPCOT is Spaceship Earth, a geodesic sphere 180 feet in diameter. Its purpose, courtesy of AT & T, is to narrate 'the dramatic history of human communications—from the earliest cave drawings to satellite technology'.

The sphere is perched on a tripod, under which you must walk to enter the park. One leg contains the entry to the exhibit. It engulfs the guests as they enter the park, and Walter Cronkite narrates as they rise up a steep incline into the sphere. History is played out, the story of writing marked by milestones such as the Rosetta Stone and, for no particular reason, Michelangelo making marks on the Sistine ceiling.[18] This narrative takes you spiralling through a good portion of the sphere, into the age of newspapers and mass communications. And, at the end of this historical ascent—this tale of the increasingly sophisticated means by which the real is knitted together—your seat suddenly swivels around to give upon 'a remarkable view of the planet we call home'.

The entire experience is reversed. Instead of being inside the globe of Spaceship Earth, you are now represented as outside, looking at the sphere of the world, which is also the product (both literally and conceptually) of the narrativising equipment through which you've just travelled. This epiphany is projected as the absolution of data that is to be achieved in the future when the whole world is available to everyone at the touch of a button , but it is really the oblivion of the world, which slips out somewhere between the great spherical pavilion and the sphere projected on its inner shell.[19]

This climax is effected breathtakingly. As you turn the last corner of the history of writing, space suddenly opens up before, above, and especially below, and you are given to gaze at a vast and apparently infinite abyss of stars in the midst of which is the tiny sphere of the planet.

It is probably the most reliable program in all of EPCOT, and it has the kind of visceral, moral force, the ability to alter the shape of one's world-historical body, that Henry Adams associated with the Virgin and the dynamo. It is the World, self-contained and figured as both the ultimate product of writing and the ultimate means of inscription, the divine spark of presence infinitely present to itself as gadgetry.

Now where is America in this metaphysics cum gizmology that I have discerned in Future World? America's canonical moment, its advent, is remembered on axis with this strangely redemptive Spaceship Earth. It is given a direct link to a singular planetary home that now figures only the possibility of the slippage between replications of itself. It is the moral force, not of raw industrial power, nor of enlightened reason, but of entertainment and replication that has its advent in the America of EPCOT Center. And the question of how one might consume such a monument remains, I think, curiously beyond both the intentions of EPCOT's designers and the language by which we tend to appropriate popular culture as ideology. The mystery of Adams' 'New American', of an identity bound up with the revelatory power of technology, remains curiously beyond our grasp. And the message of EPCOT Center, if any, is that the identity of any New American will be intimately conjoined with a tactics of imaging and framing multiple identities not against the ground of the world but against a newly-founded paradise of enclosed replications.

HELEN GRACE

10 Business, pleasure narrative: *The folktale in our times*

> Money demands constant vigilance. To become poor, one only has to let oneself go. But to enrich oneself requires greed. Our relationship to money demands a tension which is not reducible to any other. It is through money that the Other confronts us. The monetary act is always aggressive.
>
> André Amar in *The Psychoanalysis of Money*[1]

Within the last few years, a noticeable shift has taken place in the layout of the business pages of daily newspapers in Australia. Some of the changes which are observable have affected the whole of the newspaper, such as the increased tendency towards a kind of television-style 'programming' layout in which we are dealing not so much with time slots but rather with 'space slots'. For example, in the *Sydney Morning Herald* each day there is a special supplement, a kind of spatial filling of the paper with material directed at specific readerships (television viewers, computer buffs, gourmets, potential tourists, investors, home renovators, followers of fashion, seekers of pleasure and weekend entertainment). Each of these consuming readerships is addressed directly, the special interest which the newspaper takes in these readerships revolving largely around the fact that they have disposable incomes, which can be delivered to advertisers. Other social groupings—potential readerships such as street kids, single parents, junkies—are not directly addressed, because they do not have large disposable incomes; they are not spoken *to* but only spoken *about*. And in another magazine section of the paper concerned with social problems they are constituted as objects of spectacle. (This section of the paper takes over from what used to be the women's pages, until feminism challenged this compartmentalisation. My interest in this chapter, however, is with the men's pages, since these have certainly remained and have in fact been extended.)

The greater the disposable income of the consuming readerships, the greater the social problems will be to which they are called upon to respond. Street kids are the current favourite and so great is the fascination with them that a local advertising industry body has recently begun a campaign to set up an inner-city refuge for them, amidst a blaze of publicity for the advertising industry.

Meanwhile, the 'social problems' (debt, current account deficits, balance of payments imbalances), which are caused in part by the level of consumption encouraged in the other 'space slots', are analysed on the editorial pages and, of course, in the business pages. They are not, however, regarded as 'social problems', a category which always implies a particular social group, the 'disadvantaged'. Instead, the effects of economic, as opposed to personal, recklessness are regarded as universal problems, responsibility for them being placed with the population at large. Such consumption-induced problems becomes everyone's responsibility, rather than the responsibility of the sector of the population for whom 'welfare' is the solution, 'welfare' in this case, of course, being provided at the level of industry assistance, subsidy, and tax concessions.

On the business pages, the visual content has recently increased and we are now confronted with dramatic graphs and charts, the drama being emphasised by the widespread use of non-zero baselines, which greatly exaggerate rises and falls. Large portraits of businessmen are also a feature of the new business pages. While it is their business dealings which have made them prominent in business circles, the use of a particular style of photography constitutes them as important to the person in the street. The newspaper photograph—which must compete with television news for impact—is part of the process of putting into circulation a set of images of power. Such images become individualised in the portrait of the businessman. In this way, the man becomes important, is recognised in the street—becomes a recognisable figure beyond the narrow confines of the business world. But representation must play another important part before this world can be seen as a place of action and excitement equivalent to a football stadium on Grand Final day.

On the surface, there is nothing to see in the business world. Deals are done in secret. The telephone is used a lot, and people talking on the telephone do not present an exciting spectacle. Columns of stock prices are less interesting to read than the telephone book and the intricacy of deals remains hidden behind dense legalistic language.

On the whole, then, no spectacle is immediately observable. So it has to be produced by emphasising, as a site of action, one particular aspect of its operation. The site chosen for this emphasis is the floor of the stock exchange. Here the constraints manifest at every other level of the business world are suspended in a frenzy of activity giving the appearance of complete chaos. The spectacle is such that visitors' galleries, where spectators as well as speculators can observe the action, are provided as part of the architecture of these sites of the arbitrariness of capital's value creation. At the time of the October 1987 stock market 'correction', photographs of the figures of hysterical floor traders represented the events to a mass audience more powerfully than did the numerical figures of falling prices, since for those who had no interest in the workings of business, it was hard to see that the paper losses being referred to were in any way real. The presence of the market and the focus on its site suggests that a freedom in the determination of value is at play—everything is out in the open, so that the value which is acquired in this process is seen as a real and natural one. Given, then, that the existence of the market is a crucial rhetorical device in maintaining the belief that freedom exists, it is hardly surprising that its site should become the centre which represents the spirit of energy, activity, virility.

We are constrained at every turn by Western philosophy's divisions—logic, ethics, aesthetics, all knowledge belonging in one or other of these categories. In this structure, there can only be a consideration of the true, the beautiful, the good. Each realm is autonomous, with its own set of concerns, its own rules. Rather than casting aside this structure altogether, I choose to work around it. Along the edges, those who scavenge for the cast-off scraps resulting from attempts to fit recalcitrant bits of information into these realms will find some rich pickings in the border skirmishes, the incursions into foreign territories which take place in these regions.

Aesthetics proper has nothing to do with logic and ethics, notwithstanding the assumption of a high-minded truth and goodness expressed by art, which is manifest amongst high cultural followers of aesthetic experience. It certainly has nothing to do with money, a distasteful substance, which does not fit into any of philosophy's knowledge categories. Money appears only as an abstraction, which does not oblige philosophy actually to handle it. (To do so would verge on usury—which itself is caught up in a long history of ambivalence and persecution.[2]) There do exist a number of key works which could be said to belong to a philosophy of money.[3] Monetary theorists, however, have no trouble with the idea of appropriating an aesthetic dimension in order to give concrete form to their own concerns:

> Monetary theory is like a Japanese garden. It has esthetic unity born of variety; an apparent simplicity that conceals a sophisticated reality; a surface view that dissolves in ever deeper perspectives. Both can be fully appreciated only if examined from many different angles, only if studied leisurely but in depth. Both have elements that can be enjoyed independently of their whole, yet attain their full realization only as part of the whole.[4]

The particular success of the Japanese economic effort renders the use of the Japanese garden metaphor all the more appropriate. My reason for quoting Friedman is to point to the ready use of language's poetic function which is made by theorists whose disciplines will have nothing to do with poetics or aesthetics on the whole. For emphasis, however, it is left to a function of *language* to produce the desired effect and to carry the power of arguments which are presented initially in forms which belong to the realm of logic rather than aesthetics.

In the title essay of the book to which I've referred here, an elaborate argument is developed to produce a formula representing the optimum quantity of money within a community. It takes into account the distinction between the nominal and the real quantity of money and the distinction between the alternatives open to the individual and those that are open to the whole community. (So here we also enter the realm of ethics, which is disallowed by aesthetics and logic.) The optimum quantity of money is expressed in the following way:

$$\mathrm{MRY} = \mathrm{IRD}(0) = r_E = -\left(\frac{\mathrm{I}}{\mathrm{P}}\frac{\mathrm{dP}}{\mathrm{bt}}\right)^*,$$

$$\mathrm{MPM} = \mathrm{MNPS}_\mathrm{M} = \mathrm{MNPS}_\mathrm{B} = r_\mathrm{B} = 0$$

Clearly, this form does not belong to a consideration of aesthetics, unless one concerns oneself with issues of typography or layout, issues which are quite extrinsic to this abstraction. What we are presented with in formulations like this is an attempt to quantify a social experience. One may approve of such an attempt, admiring its elegance, or one may regard it as somehow missing the point of the social, an argument which is often locked into a romantic view of social experience as being beyond representation. Either way, the dominance of quantitative research is well established, for reasons which are accounted for in simple, seemingly innocent assertions such as: '. . . modern man likes to measure',[5] itself a displacement of another more subjective explanation, which always remains hidden from these speculations—that is, modern man *is* the measure of all things.

But it is also too simplistic to dismiss a formulation like this as being concerned entirely with the quantification of social experience. Another function is at play here which is of more importance to us—the desire to produce a model which represents what is described. A displacement, a representation. Whenever a model is built and applied, there is a sense in which we enter a structure of similarities and contrasts, or in other words, language and metaphor. This structure, in a certain way, is accounted for by the category which Foucault calls the classical episteme, in which a reflective model of reality applies:

> Up to the end of the sixteenth century, resemblance played a constructive role in the knowledge of Western culture. It was resemblance that largely guided exegesis and the interpretation of texts; it was resemblance that organised the play of symbols, made possible knowledge of things visible and invisible and controlled the art of representing them . . . Painting imitated space. And representation—whether in the service of pleasure or of knowledge—was posited as a form of repetition; the theatre of life or the mirror of nature, that was the claim made by all language, its manner of declaring its existence and of formulating its right of speech.[6]

In those fields called the hard sciences and in the area of proper knowledge, it seems that this classical mode is still current, at a certain level, and repetition, notwithstanding its bad press in the debate with difference, returns endlessly.

Money is like desire and, these days, probably more interesting. Money is desired, not for its own sake solely, but because of its abstract value—that for which it can be exchanged. Increasingly what it is exchanged for is not a positive value, an object, a commodity, but, more likely, its own negation—debt. Money is used to buy debt. Its very absence renders it desirable for its own sake. It is the classic fetish in many ways because it stands for something else, it replaces the object which it ostensibly represents. It displaces its own referent. It becomes pure signifier, replacing its signified. In the process, money ceases to exist. Most money economies are today run on debt.

Here I am conflating Freud's and Marx's ideas on fetishism, although, on the whole, I think Marx is probably more useful to my analysis. More recently, however, a new dimension of anxiety has been added to the problem of money and debt, which perhaps adds to the value of a psychoanalysis of the economy. This is the problem of 'contagion'. Contagion occurs when investors, in assessing credit risk, group together corporations by nationality, management style or financial structure. If one such corporation fails, then all others like it may be affected, having a harder time on the financial markets.[7]

In Freud's absurdist story, we understand that fetishism is the end-result of a process of disavowal, in which a discomforting reality is displaced and condensed onto another object. The originary, primal instance of disavowal is the encounter with the reality of the absence of the maternal phallus, itself a displacement of the (boy) child's fundamental fear of castration. The fetish object takes many forms, one of the most interesting and problematic being the phallic woman, a figure in which an absence is replaced by the very form of the absent object, so that the body of woman becomes phallus. As women have entered certain sectors of the workforce, a certain anxiety seems to have emerged and a displacement of woman as representation of desire and pleasure has begun to take place. Increasingly, the sex objects are men, partly in terms of their bodily attributes but partly also because of what might be called their mind attributes; the bright young executive or bond dealer, who outsmarts the competition.

Man, as we know, is a rational creature, whereas woman is not, strictly speaking. She always stands outside reason. As the oft-quoted Archbishop Whately once put it; 'Woman is an irrational animal which pokes the fire from the top'.[8] Women become hysterical. Hysteria, after all, is named after the body of woman. Its symptoms include amnesia; *attitudes passionelles*; feelings of cold; *cephalalagia adolescentum*; deafness; *délire ecmnésique*; neck cramps; *idées fixes*; palpitations; disturbances of smell and speech; stammer, stupor; tears; throat constriction; tremor; disturbance of vision—to mention only those of particular relevance on the floor of the stock exchange.

Although woman is associated with hysteria, it is man whom we most see in states of morbid excitement; all of the symptoms mentioned are now most often to be found on sporting fields or amongst floor traders. (It is worth noting that even in Charcot's time, the most dramatic of the hysterics were men.) Notwithstanding all the knowledge we now have of woman, all the work which women have done themselves to solve the problem which was never theirs to begin with, it is man who remains the great mystery, and it is his world which is filled with the most bizarre rituals, posing as reality. One enters as a fascinated anthropologist (literally).

Let us then consider that realm of absolute reality—the world of economic reality. But we find that, in reality—if there is such a place—we are dealing with fictional entities: futures trading (commodities which do not yet exist); junk bonds (which symbolise the only logic which operates in this field of danger—the greater the risk, the greater the return, *if* there is a return at all); something which is called credit, but which is in fact, debt; and the problem of what the banks refer to as LDCs (less developed countries)—the terrifying reality of Third World Debt, in which, in a movement of the most profound poetic justice, the entire economic system of the Western world is threatened because of its enthusiasm for creating debt in order to extend credit.

Clearly, then, a world of high fiction is observable, a daily soap opera, full of the most extreme occurrences. Everyday economic life has become a fiction of terrifying realism, a horror scenario with such convincing special effects that, at times, you really feel you too are there, in the middle of it.

One of the tools for analysing economic reality might be through the insights of structural analysis of narrative, in which a common language can be identified. To apply a descriptive or analytic system in this way appeals as a means of breaking out of the entirely personalised description of occurrences which the business pages produce. These pages give a sense of uniqueness to every individual occurrence within the world of business, regardless of the repetitive monotony with which operations are carried out from one corporation to another, or from one businessman to another. Such an analysis will make it possible to deconstruct the seriousness and self-importance of the world of business and to bring to bear a certain skepticism about its claim to so much attention. Propp's *Morphology of the Folk Tale*[9] contains a useful method of analysis to apply to what might be identified as the narrative structure of the business pages, because in this context we are dealing with folktales (although not precisely in the sense in which Propp understood them)—urban myths in which villains abound and heroes and princesses may also appear in the unfolding stories which are serialised daily.

My application of Propp's structure is only partial, since his analysis is complex, and I have only attempted to apply the spheres of action of the *dramatis personae* rather than the full list of 31 functions of the characters, although this could certainly be attempted. To this extent, my application of Propp could be said to be concerned more with the anatomy rather than the physiology of the narrative, since I merely identify certain major players, without describing their functions in relation to each other in great depth. As might be expected, the narrative we are dealing with is not hermetic, so that it is not a perfect one; in particular, it is never resolved because, of course, it remains unfinished. This means that certain spheres of action predominate, especially that of villainy, and the identity of the real hero remains unclear. This is a distortion which ultimately limits the applicability of Propp's structure.

My application of the structure is also limited to—or, rather, governed by—the photographs appearing on the business pages, which, in my view, suggest the possibility of describing a classical narrative, one which is cinematic or televisual, rather than literary.

It is this cinematic or televisual aspect of the narrative, based on a heightened realism, which allows for a dissolution of boundaries between fiction and reality, so that a continuity between representation and 'real life' is made possible. To illustrate this, in November 1985, businessman Alan Bond's daughter was married in an excessive public spectacle in Perth. A church was redecorated for the event; a floating dance floor was installed on the Swan River. The event was *produced* like a Hollywood movie, with sets built, and prepublicity arranged. The event was not actually televised live, as a royal wedding would be, although national news programs picked up the story. Two days later, on the local Channel 9 (owned by Bond) an episode of 'Dynasty' was televised, which featured the remarriage of Crystal to Blake, in a televisual spectacle equalled only by the Bond wedding. One event was displaced onto the other in a basic metonymic structure.

In Propp's classic narrative analysis, seven spheres of action of the main *dramatis personae* are identified: the spheres of action of the *villain*, the *donor* or *provider*, the *helper*, a *princess* (or sought-after person) and of her father, the *dispatcher*, the *hero* and the *false hero*. If we now briefly consider some of the functions of the *dramatis personae* it becomes clear that we are concerned only with the early part of the folktale.

Here, functions numbered two to six by Propp have some applicability within the narrative of the business pages:

II *An interdiction is addressed to the hero.* Don't borrow beyond your capacity to repay, or don't pay too much for assets.

III *The interdiction is violated.* Expansion in the present market requires extensive capital, which, for companies which are not blue-chip, may only be raised through considerable risk-taking—the selling of, for example, junk bonds, which, of course, are imaginary scenarios.

IV *The villain makes an attempt at reconnaissance.* A meeting is sought to discuss matters of mutual interest and the possibility of a merger.

V *The villain receives information about his victim.* Insider trading is engaged in, which weakens the position of the hero.

VI *The villain attempts to deceive his victim in order to take possession of him or of his belongings.* The leveraged buyout or hostile takeover; the hero's companies provide cash flow and are asset-stripped.

End of the first part of the story. Break for advertisements. Or, if it's a mini-series, end of the first two hours, followed by a preview of tomorrow night's episode.

The second part of the story is, of course, only a partial narrative:

the hero and the villain join in direct combat (Function XVI); the hero reappears, after great vicissitudes, having been discredited or branded (XVII), and the villain is defeated (XVIII). The initial misfortune or lack is liquidated (XIX)—legal challenges may have proved successful, for example. The law can sometimes function as a magical agent in this story. The hero returns (XXI) but is still pursued by the past (XXII). Before being fully restored to heroic status, he must prove himself, in, for example, another country (XXIII), undertaking a particularly difficult task—for example, the restructure of a group of companies or strike-breaking, in which the unions are defeated in court (XXV). As a result, the hero acquires a new appearance; builds a marvellous palace; puts on new garments; is shown to have a sense of humour, and to be a man of the people; all is forgiven (XXIX). The villain is punished—placed in receivership (XXX), and the hero is married and ascends the throne (XXXI). This final stage of the story is much more fanciful, and aspects of it never appear on the business pages, although some parts may be dealt with in the social pages, or in gossip columns. (There is also a gossip column in the business pages, in which rumours can be put into circulation, resulting in bigger stories being developed—and more circulation for the newspaper.)

While this narrative is taking place, photography plays a role in defining the characters. Always a popular character, the *villain* and his sphere of action are not too difficult to establish, and he is the most readily identifiable of the characters in the story. He may be recognised according to his political persuasion. Paul Keating and Simon Crean might be regarded as villains for one side, John Elliott, Rupert Murdoch and Alan Bond for the other. On the business pages of a daily newspaper like the *Herald*, however, the Elliott–Murdoch–Bond group is more likely to be presented as villain, Elliott, because photograhically he *looks* like a villain, a thug—or an especially rough and tough rugby league player (there is always an ambivalence at play between villainy and heroism), Murdoch since he represents the competition for the Fairfax press, and Bond, who, at the time that this photography was being studied (1988), was in a fierce legal battle with the Fairfax proprietors over financial advice (given to Warwick Fairfax, in his attempt to finance the takeover of the *Herald* from the rest of the Fairfax family).

The images of Bond have undergone a noticeable change and the process of transformation into villainy is observable over a period of years. From images of the affable businessman, national hero and winner of the America's Cup in 1983, Bond begins to be represented as the belligerent manipulator of the media, in his disputes with for example the Broadcasting Tribunal. Political conspiracy is suggested photographically (Figure 1) by association. In this photograph, taken

Figure 1 Neville Wran and Alan Bond. *Photo courtesy of Palani Mohan and John Fairfax Group*

Figure 2 Patricia Cross, banker. *Photo courtesy of Stephen Holland and John Fairfax Group*

at the funeral of Larrie Adler (a prominent businessman who died suddenly of a heart attack in early 1989) a passing moment becomes a decisive one. Two important men, Alan Bond and former Premier Neville Wran, are shown together. It is almost a forensic picture, taken from a considerable distance with a telephoto lens. This is suggested not only by the grain of the image, but also by the fact that a smaller section of the frame has been greatly enlarged for emphasis. The photograph was carried on the front page of the business section, reproduced on a large scale. It is a suggestive photograph, indicating perhaps that Bond has friends in high places who will look after him, friends in the Labor Party, no less. The link, an accidental one, an arbitrary one, is made by pure association, but once made, implies a great deal, suggesting that something sinister is at play in the relations between Bond and his business associates and social contacts. This is a reading based on *photographic* details: grain size, image cropping, image size, lighting, depth of field and so on. Bond has also been represented as the archetypal fat capitalist, an image reminiscent of 1930s political art (Heartfield and Eisenstein). Taken from a vocabulary which is no longer considered to have currency in left cultural discourse, such an image can be used with no difficulty and without self-consciousness by the conservative press in the late 1980s. Finally, the caricature is completed when the figure becomes illustrated as a cartoon.

The sphere of action of the *donor* or provider is also represented by association. In the narrative indicated above, the State becomes the donor, providing the hero with a magical agent (money, a deal, a joint venture). But material assistance at this level is not enough—misfortune or lack has to be liquidated. The hero has to be transfigured, and in this narrative this happens through the operation of influence: social acceptance and the company of politicians who hold power. For example, a photograph has appeared on the business pages of a daily newspaper with a caption reading 'Labor's WA business friends' showing the Prime Minister and the Western Australian Labor Premier surrounded by prominent businessmen. This represents the sphere of action of the *helper* and also operates through association.

Some interest is added to the narrative by the sphere of action of a *princess* (Figure 2), or sought-after person, and of *her father*. Photographs of women are rare on the business pages and when they do appear, that presence is marked. In this example, the subject of the photograph is a merchant banker, but this is of less interest to us than the style of photography deployed, since it clearly marks out *difference* from the representations of powerful men. Femininity becomes a kind of ambivalent strength in this context. A photograph like this is so different on the business pages that it alerts us to something else at play. One might take a simplistic view and conclude that this 'something else' is merely sex. But such a reading is problematic because it assumes that women are only permitted to enter these spheres because of their physical rather than their intellectual attributes, which is simply not the case. The economic commentator, Max Walsh, has derived some of the authority of his discourse, at least in his television shows, from the presence of powerful women, who are smart, confident and knowledgeable.[10] However, the photograph undercuts the possibility of such power: a certain aloofness (achieved photographically) soft waves, a gesture of the hand, all speak desire rather than authority—the sought-after person. It was in trying to understand what this photograph is doing on the business pages that I first began to consider the possibilities of constructing a narrative analysis of the images, since it was the style of photography rather than the expertise of the subject which stood out so startlingly.

In Propp's structure, the sphere of action of the princess is continuous with that of her father: 'The princess and her father cannot be exactly delineated from each other according to functions. Most often it is the father who assigns difficult tasks due to hostile feeling toward the suitor.'[11] However, in our narrative, there is no father. This is a world of younger men, smart young men like the Charlie Sheen character in *Wall Street*—lean, hungry and prepared to do anything. Older men are displaced by the young; patricide is implicit. The father figure is either a caricature, like the representations of Reagan as Mickey Mouse, or a paternal function is taken on at the level of the sign, so that glasses, perched on the nose, or prematurely grey hair may sometimes signify mature authority. The sphere of action of the *dispatcher* may be arbitrarily attributed to a figure like Sir Peter Abeles, owner of an airline and dispatcher of the pilots' union.

The most problematic sphere of action is that of the *hero*. Notwithstanding the fact that our narrative is dependent on a hero, in fact there are no really clear candidates for this position. This is perhaps the paradox of our story. As noted earlier, it is not difficult to find a villain for the story, but at any point any possible hero can be turned into a villain. The hero does not exist (or cannot be clearly delineated from the villain, who in turn cannot be delineated from the *false hero*) because of a crisis which belongs to ethics rather than aesthetics. This crisis was expressed locally with the appointment of a new head at the Australian Graduate School of Management in 1988 and the admission that the AGSM was engaged in what has been described as 'a low-key search for someone to teach ethics' rather than leveraged buyouts.[12] 'The entrepreneur's day of leveraged growth has passed . . . because the big banks were the only ones with enough money to fund it, and they're no longer willing to lend. "You can't play the game without any chips."'[13] The business community and business students don't want to know about innovative balance sheets anymore, it seems. Harvard has been given $20 million to fund a school of ethics and now everyone wants one. Opportunities for philosophy graduates have, as a consequence, never looked better (or worse).

Endnotes

Introduction

1 Julian Barnes *Flaubert's Parrot* London: Picador, 1985, p. 38

2 Samuel Weber 'Ambivalence: The humanities and the study of literature' in *Institution and Interpretation* Minneapolis: University of Minnesota Press, 1987, p. 152

3 See Rodolphe Gasché's discussion of the misunderstanding of deconstruction evinced in some contemporary literary criticism, in *The Tain of the Mirror* Cambridge and London: Harvard University Press, 1986, p. 255, which helps to account for the current criticism of deconstruction as conservative.

4 See Jacques Derrida 'The Principles of Reason: the university in the eyes of the pupils' *Diacritics* 13:3, 1983

1: Richard Rorty and the poet's utopia

1 Richard Rorty *Contingency, Irony and Solidarity* Cambridge: Cambridge University Press, 1989

2 For an enlightened discussion of these issues, see Richard Bernstein 'Pragmatism, pluralism and the healing of wounds' in *Proceedings and Addresses of The American Philosophical Association* 63, Newark: University of Delaware, November 1989

3 'This process of coming to see other human beings as "one of us" . . . is a matter of detailed description . . . This is a task not for theory but for genres such as ethnography, the journalist's report, the comic book, the docudrama, and, especially, the novel.' Rorty, p. xvi

4 See John Searle *Expression and Meaning* Cambridge: Cambridge University Press, 1979, p. 74. I pursue this argument in 'Xenophobia: At the border of philosophy and literature' in Richard Freadman and Lloyd Reinhardt (eds) *On Literary Theory and Philosophy: A cross-disciplinary encounter* London: Macmillan, forthcoming.

5 Some recent feminist critiques have explored the political effects of using this model of the individual. See, for example, Moira Gatens'

paper 'Corporeal representation and/in the body politic' in this volume, and Marian Tapper 'Can a feminist be a liberal?' in *Australasian Journal of Philosophy* 64, 1986, supplement, pp. 37–47.

6 As, for example, when Cornel West quotes C. I. Lewis in an afterword on 'The Politics of American Neo-Pragmatism' (in John Rajchman and Cornel West (eds) *Post-Analytic Philosophy* New York: Columbia University Press, 1985, p. 259): 'Pragmatism could be characterized as the doctrine that all problems are at bottom problems of conduct.' See Rorty's paper, 'Solidarity or Objectivity?', also in that volume.

7 See, for example, 'Philosophy as a Kind of Writing', in *Consequences of Pragmatism* Minneapolis: University of Minnesota Press, 1982; 'Deconstruction and Circumvention' *Critical Inquiry* 11; 1984, pp. 1–23; 'Is Derrida a Transcendental Philosopher?' *Yale Journal of Criticism* 2:2, 1989, pp. 207–218; and 'Two Meanings of Logocentrism: A reply to Norris' in Reed Way Dasenbrock (ed) *Redrawing the Lines: Analytic Philosophy, Deconstruction and Literary Theory* Minneapolis: University of Minnesota Press, 1989, pp. 204–16. See Christopher Norris in that volume, 'Philosophy as *Not* Just a "Kind of Writing": Derrida and the claim of Reason', to which Rorty's paper is a reply.

8 Rorty *Contingency, Irony and Solidarity* p. xiv

9 ibid., p. xv

10 ibid., p. xv

11 ibid., p. 7

12 ibid., pp. 33–4

13 For an elaboration of an argument for the significance of sexual difference in the Oedipus complex see my 'Life-threatening Life: Angela Carter and the Uncanny' in *The Illusion of Life*, Sydney: Power Institute of Fine Art, 1990. See also, Teresa de Lauretis' discussion in 'Desire in narrative' *Alice Doesn't: Feminism, Semiotics, Cinema* Bloomington: Indiana University Press, 1984, pp. 103–58. Generally, de Lauretis' notion of a 'technology of gender' is an illuminating feminist rendering of theories of representation and psychoanalytic theory; see her *Technologies of Gender: Essays on Theory, Film and Fiction* London: MacMillan, 1987.

14 Rorty, *Contingency, Irony and Solidarity*, p. 7

15 Frustration with the 'free market' behind the 'free play' has been expressed recently by Christopher Norris in 'Postmodernising History: Right Wing Revisionism and the Uses of Theory', *Southern Review* 21:2, 1988, pp. 123–40; and Richard Bernstein in'One Step Forward, Two Steps Backward: Richard Rorty on Liberal Democracy and Philosophy' in *Political Theory* 15:4, 1987, pp. 538–63. See also Rorty's reply in the same issue. Of course, Marxist approaches have met a more sophisticated variety of the same difficulty in the attempt to account for the ideological power of the text within a model that privileges the economic as base.

16 Rorty, p. 9

17 ibid., p. 9

18 ibid., p. xv

19 ibid., p. xvi

20 An alternative enters post-structuralism through the work of Emmanuel Levinas. See, for example, Richard A. Cohen (ed.) *Face To Face With Levinas* New York: SUNY Press, 1986
21 Rorty, p. 35
22 ibid., p. 39
23 ibid., p. 39
24 For presentations of this argument, see Samuel Weber 'The Debts of Deconstruction and Other, Related Assumptions' in *Institution and Interpretation* Minneapolis: University of Minnesota Press, 1987; Rosalyn Diprose 'Nietzsche, Ethics and Sexual Difference' *Radical Philosophy* 52, 1989, pp. 27–33.
25 For a succinct discussion of the question of *différance*, see Jacques Derrida '*Différance*' *Margins of Philosophy* Alan Bass (trans.) Chicago: University of Chicago Press, 1982, pp. 1–28.

2: Desiring production itself: Notes on the invention of photography

1 Derrida describes the situation as far as writing is concerned as follows;

> The grammatologist least of all can avoid questioning himself about the essence of his object in the form of a question of origin: 'What is writing?' means 'where and when does writing begin?' The responses generally come very quickly. They circulate within concepts that are seldom criticized and move within evidence which always seems self-evident. It is around these responses that a typology of and a perspective on the growth of writing are always organized. All works dealing with the history of writing are composed along the same lines: a philosophical and teleological classification exhausts the critical problems in a few pages; one passes next to an exposition of facts. We have a contrast between the theoretical fragility of the reconstructions and the historical, archeological, ethnological, philosophical wealth of information.

See Jacques Derrida *Of Grammatology* Gayatri Spivak (trans.) Baltimore: Johns Hopkins University Press, 1976, p. 28

2 Daguerre had in fact made confident but premature announcements of his invention in the Parisian press during 1835 and 1838, but Arago's speech is usually taken to be photography's official launch day.
3 Helmut Gernsheim *The Origins of Photography* London: Thames and Hudson, 1982, p. 6
4 Michel Foucault *The Archaeology of Knowledge* A. M. Sheridan Smith (trans.) New York: Pantheon Books, 1972, p. 144
5 Pierre Harmant 'Anno Lucis 1839: 1st part' *Camera* 5, May 1977, p. 39, and 'Anno Lucis 1839: 3rd part' *Camera* 10, October 1977, p. 40
6 As early as 8 June 1839, the English journal *The Athenaeum* was complaining that: '. . . hardly a day passes that we do not receive letters respecting some imagined discovery or improvement in the art of photogenic drawing.' As quoted in R. Derek Wood 'J. B. Reade, F. R. S., and the early history of photography: Part 1, A re-assessment on the discov-

ery of contemporary evidence' *Annals of Science* 27:1, March 1971, pp. 13–45

7 In his 1839 paper to the Royal Society, 'Some Account of the Art of Photogenic Drawing', Talbot reminds us that there may well have been numerous proto-photographers whose names and aspirations have not come down to us. 'I have been informed by a scientific friend that this unfavourable result of Mr WEDGWOOD'S and Sir HUMPHRY DAVY'S experiments, was the chief cause which discouraged him from following up with perseverance the idea which he had also entertained of fixing the beautiful images of the *camera obscura*.' Talbot's paper is reproduced in Beaumont Newhall *Photography: Essays and Images* London: Secker & Warburg, 1980, p. 24.

8 Niépce wrote to Daguerre on 4 June 1827, as quoted in Victor Fouque *The Truth Concerning the Invention of Photography: Nicéphore Niépce, his Life, his Endeavours, his Works* Paris: Library of Authors and of the Academy of Booklovers, 1867 [Reprint Edition 1973, Arno Press, New York], p. 72. Daguerre sent Niépce his letter on 3 February 1828, as quoted in Beaumont Newhall *Latent Image: The Discovery of Photography* Albuquerque: University of New Mexico Press, 1967, p. 34.

9 Henry Fox Talbot 'Some Account of the Art of Photogenic Drawing', 31 January 1839, as reproduced in Newhall *Photography: Essays and Images* p. 25

10 William Gilpin, as quoted in Timothy Brownlow *John Clare and Picturesque Landscape*, Oxford: Clarendon Press, 1983, p. 12. Brownlow argues that in this passage Gilpin, 'uses his eye like a cine-camera'.

11 Gilpin *Forest Scenery*, 1791, as quoted in Malcolm Andrews *The Search for the Picturesque: Landscape Aesthetics and Tourism in Britain 1760–1800* Aldershot: Scolar Press, 1989, p. 70. The Claude Glass was a tinted convex mirror, usually held in the hand and commonly used in the eighteenth century to produce a darkened, reflected image of landscape reminiscent of the paintings of Claude Lorrain.

12 William Cowper, as quoted in Jean H. Hagstrum *The Sister Arts: The Tradition of Literary Pictorialism and English Poetry from Dryden to Gray* Chicago and London: University of Chicago Press, 1958, p. 139

13 Humphry Davy 'An Account of a method of copying Paintings upon Glass etc' *Journals of the Royal Institution* Vol. 1, London 1802, as reproduced in R. B. Litchfield *Tom Wedgwood: The First Photographer* London: Duckworth, 1903, p. 189.

14 Henry Fox Talbot 'Some Account of the Art of Photographic Drawing' in Newhall *Photography: Essays and Images* p. 25

15 Coleridge 'Defects and Beauties of Wordsworth's Poetry', 1817, as reproduced in Jack Davis (ed.) *Discussions of William Wordsworth* Boston: D. C. Heath, 1964, p. 7.

16 John Clare, 1824–25, as quoted in Brownlow *John Clare and Picturesque Landscape* p. 13.

17 John Constable, 1833, as reproduced in R. B. Beckett (ed.) *John Constable's Discourses* Ipswich: Suffolk Records Society, 1970, pp. 9–10.

Further examples of a poetic desire to photograph are reproduced in my article 'Burning with Desire', *Afterimage* 17:6 January 1990, pp. 8–11.

18 Arago, in his speech to the Academie des Sciences on 7 January 1839; as reproduced in Helmut and Alison Gernsheim *L. J. M. Daguerre: The History of the Diorama and the Daguerreotype* New York: Dover Publications, 1968, p. 82

19 Arago, in his Report to the Chamber of Deputies on 6 July 1839; as reproduced in *An Historical and Descriptive Account of the various Processes of the Daguerreotype and the Diorama by Daguerre* London: McLean, 1839 [Krauss Reprint Co., New York, 1969], p. 14. Not all observers greeted the onset of this 'ardent desire' with Arago's enthusiasm. As one German clergyman is said to have exclaimed: 'The wish to capture evanescent reflections is not only impossible, as has been shown by thorough German investigation, but the mere *desire* alone, the will to do so, is blasphemy.' (my emphasis) Quoted in Gernsheim *The Origins of Photography*, p. 50.

20 Michel Foucault *The Order of Things: An Archaeology of Human Sciences* New York: Vintage Books, 1973, p. 238

21 Watling's publication is reproduced in full as part of Ross Gibson's article 'This Prison this Language: Thomas Watling's *Letters from an Exile at Botany-Bay* (1794)', in Paul Foss (ed.) *Island in the Stream: Myths of Place in Australian Culture* Sydney: Pluto Press, 1988, pp. 4–28.

22 Gibson, ibid., p. 24

23 Victor Burgin, in Geoffrey Batchen 'For an Impossible Realism: An Interview with Victor Burgin' *Afterimage* 16:7, November 1989, pp. 4–5

24 Foucault *Power/Knowledge* Colin Gordon (ed.), Brighton: Harvester Press, 1980, p. 113

25 Foucault *The Order of Things* p. xi

26 Foucault *Power/Knowledge* p. 211

27 ibid., pp. 195–6

28 Foucault *The Order of Things* pp. 318–9

29 ibid., p. xxiii

30 Foucault *Discipline and Punish: The Birth of the Prison* Alan Sheridan (trans.) London: Penguin, 1977, pp. 202–3, 216

31 This particular version of what is a common misreading of Foucault, comes from Patricia R. Zimmerman 'Our Trip to Africa: Home Movies as the Eyes of the Empire' *Afterimage* 17:8, March 1990, p. 4. See also my critique of John Tagg's instrumental view of photography in 'Photography, Power, and Representation' *Afterimage* 16:4, November 1988, pp. 7–9.

32 Foucault *Discipline and Punish* pp. 202–3

33 Foucault *Power/Knowledge* p. 98

34 Niépce, 1832, as quoted in Aaron Scharf *Pioneers of Photography: an album of pictures and words* London: British Broadcasting Corporation, 1975, p. 35.

35 Daguerre, c. 1838, as quoted in Helmut and Alison Gernsheim *L.J.M. Daguerre: The History of the Diorama and the Daguerreotype* p. 81.

36 Talbot, this being the full title of his 1839 paper to the Royal Society, as reproduced in Newhall *Photography: Essays and Images* p. 23

37 Chris Titterington 'Construction and Appropriation' in Mike Weaver (ed.) *The Art of Photography* London: The Royal Academy of the Arts, 1989, p. 424

38 It is interesting to note that in his influential book *The Mirror and The Lamp*, M. H. Abrams describes a parallel hesitation he sees as inhabiting the field of poetry at this same time. 'The title of the book identifies two common and antithetic metaphors of mind, one comparing the mind to a reflector of external objects, the other to a radiant projector which makes a contribution to the object it perceives.'

See M. H. Abrams *The Mirror and The Lamp: Romantic Theory and the Critical Tradition* New York: Norton, 1953, p. viii

39 Foucault *Power/Knowledge* p. 97

40 Niépce, 1816, as quoted in Beaumont Newhall *The History of Photography, from 1839 to the Present Day* New York: Museum of Modern Art, 1949, p. 12

41 Foucault *Power/Knowledge* p. 186

42 See Paul Patton 'Notes for a glossary' *Ideology & Consciousness* 8, 1981, pp. 41–48

43 Gilles Deleuze and Félix Guattari *Anti-Oedipus: Capitalism and Schizophrenia* Minneapolis: University of Minnesota Press, 1983, pp. 26, 29

44 Deleuze and Guattari *A Thousand Plateaus: Capitalism and Schizophrenia* Minneapolis: University of Minnesota Press, 1987, p. 399.

45 Foucault 'Nietzsche, Genealogy, History' in Donald F. Bouchard (ed.) *Language, Counter-Memory, Practice* Ithaca: Cornell University Press, 1977, p. 142

3: Dot, circle, difference: Translating Central Desert paintings

1 Judith Ryan *Mythscapes: Aborginal Art of the Desert* Exhibition Catalogue Melbourne: National Gallery of Victoria, 1989, p. 6

2 Warlukurlangu Artists *Kuruwarri: Yuendumu Doors* Canberra: Australian Institute of Aboriginal Studies, 1987

3 John von Sturmer has since identified the politics of representation as the single issue for Aborigines in the 1980s, arguing that it is necessary to separate the issue of Aboriginal control of the production of their representations from the consequences of their circulation, in 'Aborigines, Representation, Necrophilia' *Art & Text* 32, Autumn 1989, pp. 127–39

4 Australian Institute of Aboriginal Studies (AIAS) 'Press Release of Warlukurlangu Artists *Kuruwarri: Yuendumu Doors*' Canberra: Australian Institute of Aboriginal Studies, August, 1987

5 Warlukurlangu Artists *Kuruwarri: Yuendumu Doors*, p. 2

6 Gayatri Spivak takes up this point in her discussion of the difficulties in translating, see 'Translators Preface' Jacques Derrida *Of Grammatology* Baltimore: John Hopkins University Press, 1974, p. lxxxvi

7 It has been pointed out to me that translations of these English texts into Warlpiri were not included as Warlpiri do not need them. It may be that Warlpiri do not 'need' the discussion of the country and sites

evoked by the text, but in what sense do they not 'need' to be informed about how Europeans discuss their paintings, their language, their country? Surely if this text were '... for Aboriginal people and not just about them' as Muecke's review states ('When 30 Doors Help Open the World to Aboriginal Dreamtime' *Times on Sunday*, September 9, 1987), it would have to take equally seriously the translation of these European deliberations back to Warlpiri.

8 See, for example, A. Brody *The Face of the Centre: Papunya Tula Paintings 1971–84* Exhibition Catalogue Melbourne: National Gallery of Victoria, 1984; J. Maughan and J. Zimmer (eds) *Dot and Circle: A Retrospective Survey of the Aboriginal Acrylic Paintings of Central Australia* Exhibition Catalogue Melbourne: Royal Melbourne Institute of Technology, 1986; Peter Sutton (ed.) *Dreamings: The Art of Aboriginal Australia* New York and Adelaide: Viking in association with The Asia Society Galleries and Penguin Books, 1988 and Judith Ryan *Mythscapes: Aboriginal Art of the Desert* Exhibition Catalogue: National Gallery of Victoria, 1989. All these texts contain, in various forms, at least partial 'stories' and 'iconographic' decipherings. Not one enlists vernacular transcripts or includes translations from the artist's language.

9 Eric Michaels 'Western Desert Sand Painting and Postmodernism' in Warlukurlangu Artists *Kuruwarri: Yuendumu Doors*, pp. 133–43. I use the marked team 'himself' here as the artists, in this case, are all male.

10 Roland Barthes 'The Photographic Image' in *Image, Music, Text* Stephen Heath (trans.) New York: Hill and Wang, 1977

11 N. D. Munn *Walbiri Iconography: Graphic Representation and Cultural Symbolism in a Central Australian Society* Ithaca and London: Cornell University Press, 1973, p. 58

12 This is granted in *Kuruwarri: Yuendumu Doors*, p. 2

13 Walter Benjamin 'The Task of the Translator: An Introduction to the Translation of Baudelaire's *Tableaux Parisiens*' in Walter Benjamin *Illuminations* Hannah Arendt (ed. and intro.) Harry Zohn (trans.) New York: Schocken Books. 1969

14 ibid., p. 69

15 ibid., p. 75

16 Paul de Man '"Conclusions" Walter Benjamin's "The Task of the Translator" Messenger Lecture, Cornell University, March 4, 1983' *Yale French Studies* 69, 1985, p. 36

17 Benjamin 'The Task of the Translator', p. 78

18 I employ de Man's translation of Benjamin here, from 'Conclusions' p. 43, in preference to that of the original English translation of Zohn's. In what is a persuasive argument, de Man indicates the impossibilities of a reproductive translation by demonstrating how very differently this text of Benjamin's has been rendered in both English and French translations.

19 ibid., pp. 43–4

20 Benjamin 'The Task of the Translator', p. 79

21 ibid., pp. 80–1

22 S. Muecke, A. Rumsey and B. Wirrunmara 'Pigeon the outlaw: history as texts *Aboriginal History* 9, 1985, pp. 81–100 and D. Tedlock *The Spoken Word and the Work of Interpretation* Philadelphia: University of Pennsylvania Press, 1983

23 While Heath, for example, offers morpheme by morpheme gloss translations between Nunggubuyu and English (in J. Heath *Nunggubuyu Myths and Ethnographic Texts* Canberra: Australian Institute of Aboriginal Studies, 1980) and involves the reader directly in an engagement with the 'foreignness of languages', it remains a literal rendering; a far cry from the type of translation proffered by Benjamin. The closest English translations of an Aboriginal language to that which Benjamin seeks, is perhaps found in Strehlow's translations from Aranda (T. G. H. Strehlow *Songs of Central Australia* Sydney: Angus & Robertson, 1971). These translations are in no sense 'reproductive', in fact are often, ironically, criticised for the extent to which they sound, in English, biblical and/or Icelandic in origin.

24 Warlukurlangu Artists *Kuruwarri: Yuendumu Doors*, p. 2

25 Australian Institute of Aboriginal Studies Press Release for Warlkurlangu Artists *Kuruwarri: Yuendumu Doors*

26 There is some indication that as a form of writing in a general or Derridean sense, these 'symbols' may operate more metonymically than metaphorically (as suggested by Eric Michaels in 'Aboriginal Media History: an Inverted Sequence' unpublished paper delivered to the Department of Sociology, University of New South Wales, 1986 and F. Dubinskas and S. Traweek in 'Closer to the Ground: a Reinterpretation of Warlpiri Iconography' *Man* 19:1, 1984, pp. 15–30). However this is a very different argument from one that posits these 'symbols' as simply iconographic substitutes for a given materiality.

27 Warlukurlangu Artists *Kuruwarri: Yuendumu Doors*, p. 4

28 For a wider discussion of this phenomenon and its consequences see Jacques Derrida *Of Grammatology* G. C. Spivak (trans.) Baltimore: Johns Hopkins University Press, 1974

29 Charles S. Peirce *The Writings of Charles S. Peirce: a Chronological Edition* Bloomington: Indiana University Press, 1982

30 Munn *Warlbiri Iconography*

31 For other discussions of these points see, for example: Michaels 'Aboriginal Media History'; Fred Myers *Pintupi Country: Pintupi Self* Canberra: Australian Institute of Aboriginal Studies, 1986; N. D. Munn 'The Transformation of Subjects into Objects in Walbiri and Pitjantjatjara Myth in M. Charlesworth (ed.) *Religion in Aboriginal Australia: An Anthology* St Lucia: University of Queensland Press, 1984, pp. 56–82 and *Walbiri Iconography*; John Morton 'Representing the Country, Disclosing the Self' a review article *Oceania* 57, pp. 304–13; Dubinkas and Traweek 'Closer to the Ground'; C. Anderson and F. Dussart 'Dreamings in Acrylic: Western Desert Art' in P. Sutton (ed.) *Dreamings: The Art of Aboriginal Australia.*

32 von Sturmer's review of P. Roe *Gularabulu: Stories from the West Kimberly* and B. Shaw *Banggaiyerri: The Story of Jack Sullivan as Told*

to Bruce Shaw in *Mankind* 15, 1985, p. 263. von Sturmer also notes elsewhere that the metaphor of 'mapping' for how Aborigines 'see' the country is one necessarily produced in a climate of mining, land rights and anthropology. That is, a metaphor dependent upon a relationship between those who know and are showing, and those who don't but are concerned to see the country 'mapped' (von Sturmer 'Aborigines, Representation, Necrophilia', p. 136).

33 As Munn notes in *Walbiri Iconography*, pp. 64, 69, 72–3. Munn claims, for example, that the story-tellers tended to verbalize '. . . more of the story when I was taking notes on it than they would have ordinarily, or than they did when I was just listening and not trying to record the account in full' (p. 72).

34 It has been pointed out to me that the actual recordings of the stories were done by Warlpiri and not by Europeans (Eric Michaels pers. comm., March 1988). However, I am not necessarily convinced that this shifts the terms of trade substantially, given the coincidence of the European drive to document the Aborigine with the Aborigines current interest in their own documentation. As the Warlukurlangu Artists state (in translation) at the beginning of the text: 'We painted these dreamings on the school doors because our children should learn about the Law . . . The children do not know them and might become like white people, which we don't want to happen' (Warlukurlangu Artists *Kuruwarri: Yuendumu Doors*, p. 1). Also, the discussion in the 'afterword' on the negotiations between the artists and AIAS indicates that the text was produced for a European audience in order to facilitate the sale of the paintings (ibid., pp. 138–9).

The extent to which the 'telling of the story' has become traditionalised in terms of European expectations is augmented in an extract from Bruce Chatwin's *The Songlines* appearing in the *Sydney Morning Herald* (22 August 1987, p. 48). Chatwin's narrative portrays a European art dealer hassling an Aboriginal artist for his painting 'story' in order to sell it to a gallery 'down south'. The Aborigine resists by basically inventing a nonsense 'story'.

35 Michel Foucault *The History of Sexuality Volume I: An Introduction* Robert Hurley (trans.) New York: Vintage/Random House, 1978, p. 162

36 Warlukurlangu Artists *Kuruwarri: Yuendumu Doors*, pp. 3, 103

37 ibid., p. 19

38 ibid., p. 127

39 ibid., p. 91

40 The term is Stephen Muecke's in 'Body, Inscription, Epistemology: Knowing Aboriginal Texts' E. S. Nelson (ed.) *Connections* Canberra: Australian Institute of Aboriginal Studies, 1988, pp. 41–52

41 See James Clifford's discussion of this particular point in relation to Said's 'Orientalism' in J. Clifford and G. E. Marcus (eds) *Writing Culture: the Poetics and Politics of Ethnography* Berkeley: University of California Press, 1986, p. 12

42 McGregor claims that the fact that English lacks a narrative genre equivalent to the Aboriginal myth or story may explain why so many of

these end up published as children's stories (William McGregor 'The structure of Gooniyandi narratives' *Australian Aboriginal Studies* 2, 1987, p. 21). Yet, von Sturmer notes (in relation to Muecke's translation of the stories of Paddy Roe in *Gularabulu: Stories from the West Kimberly* Fremantle: Fremantle Arts Centre Press, 1983) that these translations can provide appreciation of the 'story event' only for 'readers who have been exposed to Aboriginal story telling' (see von Sturmer's review in *Mankind* 15, 1985, p. 264).

43 For Derrida's account of *différance* as the precondition and remainder of an oppositional 'economy of difference' see, for example, 'Différance' in *Margins of Philosophy* Alan Bass (trans.) Chicago: University of Chicago Press, 1982

44 Fry and Willis have recently linked the Australian national obsession with landscape and with the non-urban 'emptiness' of the desert, to the success of Central Desert paintings. This 'emptiness', this quest for national identity (underscored by recent Bicentennial celebrations) has been filled, in part, by Central Desert art. These paintings stand for a continuity in this identity and have had the international success necessary to be appreciated fully by their 'own' country. However, Fry and Willis' reductive conclusions that exploitation and commercialism are the operant terms of the paintings' success belie the paintings salience. These paintings do have 'something to say', as Thomas points out in his critical response to Fry and Willis; something which may resonate with, but cannot be reduced to, a commodification of national identity. (Tony Fry and Anne-Marie Willis 'Criticism Against the Current' *Meanjin* 48:2, 1989, pp. 223–240 and Martin Thomas 'Identity as a Lost Cause' *Art & Text* 35, Summer 1990, pp. 87–95)

45 von Sturmer 'Aborigines, Representation, Necrophilia', p. 129

46 Michaels 'Western Desert Sandpaintings', p. 135

47 ibid., pp. 141–43

48 Not one of these art texts (cf. footnote 8 above) fails to mention the resemblance of Central Desert paintings to that of Western abstract modernism. For example, Anderson and Dussart: 'To some extent, though, the acceptance of desert acrylics is due to the art's remarkable similarities to Western abstract painting' (Anderson and Dussart 'Dreamings in Acrylic', p. 90). But this passage is qualified in case the reader assumes that the Desert artists have knowledge of Western art history: '. . . most of the artists are non-literate and rarely travel beyond their remote homes' (p. 127f.). This pivot between paintings that do resemble and are identifiable (as modernism) and simultaneously artists who don't resemble, who aren't simply identified (as the modern artist), accounts less for the paintings 'acceptance' to the European than their *raison d'etre*.

49 On the role of the 'supplement' see Derrida *Of Grammatology*. On the uncertain role of the signature see Derrida, 'Signature, Event, Context' Samuel Weber and Jeffrey Mehlman (trans.) *Glyph* 1, 1977, pp. 172–97, also published in *Margins of Philosophy*.

50 Sutton (ed.) *Dreamings: The Art of Aboriginal Australia*

51 *The Weekend Australian* Magazine 6, August 8–9, 1987

4: Nietzsche and the body of the philosopher

1 Alexander Nehamas *Nietzsche: Life as Literature* Cambridge, Massachusetts: Harvard University Press, 1985, p. 23
2 Nietzsche *The Gay Science* paragraph 216, W. Kaufmann (trans.) New York: Random House, 1974, p. 210
3 Nietzsche *Beyond Good and Evil* paragraph 40, R. J. Hollingdale (trans.) London: Penguin, 1973, p. 51
4 Nietzsche *On The Genealogy of Morals/ Ecce Homo* W. Kaufmann and R. J. Hollingdale (trans.) New York: Random House, 1967, p. 219
5 Nietzsche *Ecce Homo* Chapter II, p. 256
6 Nietzsche *On the Genealogy of Morals* Third Essay, section 7, p. 107
7 Gilles Deleuze *Spinoza: Practical Philosophy* Robert Hurley (trans.) San Francisco: City Lights Books, 1988, p. 127
8 Gilles Deleuze and Felix Guattari *A Thousand Plateaus* Brian Massumi (trans.) Minneapolis: University of Minnesota Press, p. 257
9 cf. Paul Patton 'Taylor and Foucault on Power and Freedom' *Political Studies* XXXVII, 1989.
10 Nietzsche *The Will to Power* paragraph 636, W. Kaufmann and R. J. Hollingdale (trans.) New York: Random House, 1968, p. 340
11 Elias Canetti *Crowds and Power* Carol Stewart (trans.) London: Penguin, 1973, chapter entitled 'The Entrails of Power'
12 Nietzsche *Beyond Good and Evil* paragraph 259, p. 175
13 cf. Carole Pateman *The Sexual Contract* Cambridge: Polity Press, 1988, chapter 5: 'Wives, Slaves and Wage Slaves'
14 Nietzsche *On the Genealogy of Morals* Preface, section 6, p. 20
15 Nietzsche *Beyond Good and Evil* paragraph 13, W. Kaufman (trans.), N.Y.: Random House, 1966, p. 21
16 Nietzsche *Thus Spoke Zarathustra* Prologue, R. J. Hollingdale (trans.) London: Penguin, 1961, p. 44
17 ibid. Part One 'Of the Way of the Creator', pp. 90–1
18 Nietzsche *Untimely Meditations* R. J. Hollingdale (trans.) Cambridge: Cambridge University Press, 1983, p. 141
19 Nietzsche *Beyond Good and Evil* paragraph 211, Hollingdale (trans.), p. 123. Kaufmann's translation has 'genuine philosophers' (p. 136), which suggests a rather different reading of this passage.
20 Nietzsche *Human, All Too Human* paragraph 618, Marion Faber (trans.) Lincoln and London: University of Nebraska Press p. 256
21 Nietzsche *Beyond Good and Evil* paragraph 43, Hollingdale, p. 53
22 Nietzsche *Thus Spoke Zarathustra* Part Three 'Of the Spirit of Gravity', p. 213
23 ibid. Part Three 'Of Old and New Law Tables', p. 226
24 Nietzsche *The Gay Science* paragraph 72, p. 129
25 Nietzsche *Thus Spoke Zarathustra* Part Four 'Of the Higher Man', p. 301
26 Nietzsche *Ecce Homo* p. 266
27 Alison Ainley '"Ideal Selfishness"—Nietzsche's Metaphor of Maternity' in *Exceedingly Nietzsche* D. F. Krell and D. Wood (eds) London: Routledge, 1988, p. 122f

28 Jacques Derrida *Spurs/Eperons* Barbara Harlow (trans.) Chicago: University of Chicago Press, p. 65
29 Nietzsche *Daybreak* paragraph 177, R. J. Hollingale (trans.) Cambridge: Cambridge University Press, 1982, p. 107
30 Nietzsche *Thus Spoke Zarathustra* Part Four 'The Sign', p. 334
31 Nietzsche *On The Genealogy of Morals* Third Essay, section 8, p. 110
32 Nietzsche *Thus Spoke Zarathustra* Part Two 'The Stillest Hour', p. 168
33 Nietzsche *On The Genealogy of Morals* Third Essay, section 8, p. 110
34 Nietzsche *Thus Spoke Zarathustra* Part One 'Of Chastity', p. 81
35 Marshall Berman, *All That Is Solid Melts Into Air*, New York: Simon & Schuster, 1982
36 Nietzsche *Human, All Too Human* paragraph 290, p. 173
37 Nietzsche *On The Genealogy of Morals* Third Essay, section 8, p. 109
38 Nietzsche *Thus Spoke Zarathustra* p. 242
39 Nietzsche *On The Genealogy of Morals* Third Essay, section 8, p. 109

5: Life itself

1 M. Classen and J. Philip 'Electronic Endoscopy of the Gastrointestinal Tract. Initial experience with a new type of endoscope that has no fiberoptic bundle for imaging' *Endoscopy* 16, 1984, pp. 16–9
2 Producer Saul David, Director Richard Fleischer, 1966
3 Phil Hardy (ed.) *Science Fiction* New York: William Morrow, 1984, p. 252
4 This is the advertised name of a video-endoscope manufactured at Fujinon.
5 Classen and Philip 'Electronic Endoscopy'
6 Produced and directed by Bo G. Erikson and Carl O. Lofman, Swedish Television Corp., 1982
7 Vesalius' *De humani corporis fabrica libri septem* (Basel, 1543), contained the first anatomical description of the entire human body.
8 Michel Foucault *The Birth of the Clinic* A. M. Sheridan Smith (trans.) New York: Random House, 1975, pp. 165–6
9 Francis Bacon *The New Organon* (1620) in F. H. Anderson (ed.) New York: Bobbs Merrill, 1960, p. 53
10 William C. Wees gives a general description of the *camera obscura* in photographic and film theory in 'The Cinematic Image As a Visualisation of Sight' *Wide Angle* 4, 3 1980, pp. 28–37.
11 Jacques Derrida argues that natural light is never subjected to radical doubt in Descartes' philosophy. Our field of vision unfolds *in* light. 'White Mythologies' in *Margins of Philosophy*, Alan Bass (trans.) Sussex: The Harvester Press, 1982, p. 267.
12 Artistotle *De Anima* II, 1,412 b5 in *The Works of Aristotle* Vol III J. A. Smith (trans.) Oxford: Clarenden Press, 1931
13 Aristotle *Historia Animalium* VIII 1 in *The Works of Aristotle* Vol IV D'Arcy Wentworth Thompson (trans.) Oxford: Clarenden Press, 1910
14 Edmund Husserl *Experience and Judgement* pp. 44–5, quoted in Jacques Derrida *Edmund Husserl's Origin of Geometry: An Introduction*

John P. Leavey, Jr (trans.) Lincoln and London: University of Nebraska Press, 1989, p. 118

15 ibid.

16 Derrida 'White Mythologies' p. 259

17 ibid., p. 264

18 ibid., fn 79, pp. 264–5

19 Gaston Bachelard *The Psychoanalysis of Fire* Alan C. M. Ross (trans.) London and New York: Quartet Books, 1987, p. 48

20 ibid.

21 Gaston Bachelard *La Formation de l'esprit scientifique*, quoted in Derrida 'White Mythologies' pp. 259–60

22 Gaston Bachelard *The Psychoanalysis of Fire* p. 60

23 ibid., p. 5

24 ibid., p. 46

25 ibid., pp. 2–3

26 Friedrich Nietzsche *The Gay Science* Walter Kaufmann (trans.) New York: Vintage Books, 1974, S 300, p. 240

27 Derrida 'White Mythologies' p. 209

28 Transcribed commentary from *The Miracle of Life*

29 Tom Gunning 'An Aesthetic of Astonishment: Early Film and the (In)-credulous Spectator' *Art & Text* 34, Spring, 1989, pp. 31–45

30 ibid., p. 36

31 This visual aspect of modern science has long been recognised and analysed. With reference to biology see, for example, Donna Haraway: 'At the very beginning of biology as a systemic study, Aristotle drew heavily on the analogy of artist, artisan and organism . . . These strongly *visualizable* forms are more than props for the imagination; they have been intrinsic to explanations of basic properties of life.' *Crystals, Fabrics, and Fields: Metaphors of Organicism in Twentieth Century Developmental Biology* New Haven and London: Yale University Press, 1976, pp. 40–2. However, my argument is that such images participate in the metaphysical determination, rather than explanation, of 'life'. Scientists are careful to emphasise that simulations are only an *aid* to the understanding of the 'real world': 'Simulations break reality into chunks, as many as possible, but always too few . . . Whenever a good physicist examines a simulation, he must wonder what bit of reality was *left out* [my emphasis].' James Gleick *Chaos: Making a New Science* London: Penguin Group, 1988, p. 210

32 Advertisements carried by *Endoscopy* in 1988

33 Gilles Deleuze 'Plato and the Simulacrum' Rosalind Krauss (trans.) *October* 27, Winter, 1983, pp. 47–56

34 Samuel Weber 'It' *Glyph* 4, 1978, p. 2

35 Aristotle *De Generatione animalium* in *The Works of Aristotle* Vol.V A. Platt (trans.) Oxford: Clarenden Press, 1912

36 ibid., p. 7

37 Quoted in John Farley *Gametes and Spores* Baltimore and London: The Johns Hopkins University Press, 1982, p. 16

38 Georges Canguilhem *La connaissance de la vie* Paris: Vrin, 1969, quoted Derrida 'White Mythologies' p. 261

39 Farley *Gametes and Spores* p. 101

40 See, for example, Nancy Tuana, 'The Weaker Seed: The Sexist Bias of Reproductive Theory' *Hypatia* 3, 1, 1988, pp. 35–59, and The Biology and Gender Study Group 'The Importance of Feminist Critique for Contemporary Cell Biology' *Hypatia* 3, 1, pp. 61–76

41 The Biology and Gender Study Group 'The Importance of Feminist Critique' p. 72

42 ibid., p. 73

43 For example, Thomas Kuhn accounts for science's existence and success in terms of evolution from a community's state of knowledge at any given time. See *The Structure of Scientific Revolutions* Chicago: The University of Chicago Press, 1962

44 Francois Jacob *The Logic of Life* New York: Vintage Books, 1976, p. 16

45 Nowhere more than in feminist critiques of sexual difference have biologistic arguments been identified and rejected on the grounds of their essentialism. As Elizabeth Grosz describes the way in which the term is generally applied in feminist theory: 'Biologism is a particular form of essentialism in which women's essence is defined in terms of their biological capacities ... Insofar as biology is assumed to constitute an unalterable bedrock of identity, the attribution of biologistic characteristics amounts to a permanent form of social containment for women.' 'A Note on Essentialism and Difference' in S. Gunew (ed.) *Feminist Knowledge: Critique and Construct* London: Routledge (forthcoming).

6: A 'genethics' that makes sense

1 Fay Weldon *The Cloning of Joanna May* London: Collins 1989, p. 120

2 For example 'ethos' is defined by Aristotle as character established through habitual action in *Nicomachean Ethics*, Book 2, Ch. 1. See also Charles Scott's detailed etymology of *ethos* in 'Heidegger and the Question of Ethics' *Research in Phenomenology* 18, 1988.

3 See, for example, the work of Luce Irigaray, particularly *Ethique de la Difference Sexuelle* Paris: Minuit, 1984; Moira Gatens 'Representation in/and the body politic' in this collection and 'Woman and Her Double(s): Sex, Gender and Ethics' *Australian Feminist Studies* 10, 1989; my reading of Nietzsche's ethics in R. Diprose 'Nietzsche, Ethics and Sexual Difference' *Radical Philosophy* 52, 1989; Rosi Braidotti 'The Politics of Ontological Difference' in Teresa Brennan (ed.) *Between Feminism and Psychoanalysis* London and New York: Routledge, 1989; Michel Foucault, particularly *The Use of Pleasure* Robert Hurley (trans.) New York: Vintage, 1985; and Emmanuel Levinas, particularly *Totality and Infinity* Alphonso Lingis (trans.) Pittsburgh: Duquesne University Press, 1969.

4 The meaning of 'Being-in' is Martin Heidegger's question in *Being and Time* John Macquarrie and Edward Robinson (trans.) New York: Harper & Row, 1962, s. 12, pp. 78–86.

5 This kind of ethics of specificity is evoked by H. Tristram Engelhardt Jr in *The Foundations of Bioethics* New York and Oxford: Oxford Uni-

versity Press, 1986 and by various papers in a special issue of *Hypatia* on feminist ethics and medicine, 4:2, 1989 without reference to the problem of embodiment (with the exception of Susan Wendell's account of disability in the latter).

6 David Schenck 'The Texture of Embodiment: Foundation for Medical Ethics' *Human Studies* 9, 1986

7 ibid., p. 44

8 ibid., p. 46

9 ibid., p. 50

10 ibid., p. 51

11 M. Merleau-Ponty *Phenomenology of Perception* Colin Smith (trans.) London: Routledge & Kegan Paul, 1962, p. 148

12 Heidegger *Being and Time*, s.12, p. 79 and s.18, pp. 114–122

13 David Suzuki and Peter Knudtson *Genethics: the Ethics of Engineering Life* Sydney: Allen & Unwin, 1989, p. 180

14 For an account of genetics, difference and AIDS see Rosalyn Diprose and Cathy Vasseleu 'Animation-AIDS and Science/Fiction' in A. Cholodenko (ed.) *The Illusion of Life* Sydney: The Power Institute, 1990. See also Donna Haraway 'The Biopolitics of Postmodern Bodies: Determinations of Self in Immune System Discourse' *Differences* 1:1, 1989

15 For documentation of this lack of consensus see D. C. Wertz and J. C. Fletcher (eds) *Ethics and Human Genetics: A Cross Cultural Perspective* Berlin: Springer-Verlag, 1989

16 Leon R. Kass 'The New Biology: What Price Relieving Man's Estate' in Richard W. Wertz (ed.) *Readings on Ethical and Social Issues in Biomedicine* New Jersey: Prentice-Hall Inc., 1973, p. 62

17 ibid.

18 Suzuki and Knudtson *Genethics*, p. 336

19 Bernard Davis, for example, defends the progress that genetics can bring by claiming that the 'misuse' of genetics is no worse than, and merely feeds into, other politically contaminated methods for regulating individuals, 'Prospects for Genetic Intervention in Man' in *Readings on Ethical and Social Issues in Biomedicine*. Charles Birch uses the same distinction between 'bad politics' and scientific exploration of reality slightly differently. He claims that the use of genetics to eliminate real differences is a virtue which rectifies inequalities resulting from the biased evaluation of genetic differences in 'wrong political and social systems'. See 'Genetics and Moral Responsibility' Charles Birch and Paul Abrecht (eds) *Genetics and the Quality of Life* Sydney: Pergamon Press, 1975, p. 8

20 This idea pervades Hegel's work but a brief account can be found in *Hegel's Logic* William Wallace (trans.) Oxford: Oxford University Press, 1975, s. 119, pp. 171–4. For an account of how Hegel's self/other relation works in regard to sexual difference see Genevieve Lloyd *The Man of Reason: 'Male' and 'Female' in Western Philosophy* London: Methuen, 1984, pp. 70–85

21 Emmanuel Levinas *Ethics and Infinity: Conversations with Philippe Nemo* Richard A. Cohen (trans.) Pittsburgh: Duquesne University Press, 1985, p. 91

22 *Genethics*, p. 52
23 ibid., p. 68
24 For Derrida's most concise account of this operation see Jacques Derrida 'Différance' in *Margins of Philosophy* Alan Bass (trans.) Chicago: University of Chicago Press, 1982. See also chapters by Vicki Kirby and Cathy Vasseleu in this collection for further discussion of the effects of this operation within the discourses of the biological sciences.
25 As Derrida claims, 'subjectivity—like objectivity—is an effect of *différance*'. Hence, there can be no subject of the difference which conditions this distinction. See Jacques Derrida, *Positions* Alan Bass (trans.) Chicago: University of Chicago Press, 1972, p. 28
26 Michel Foucault *The History of Sexuality Volume I* Robert Hurley (trans.) New York: Random House, 1978, pp. 135–45
27 Aldous Huxley *Brave New World* Harmondsworth: Penguin, 1955, p. 7

7: Corporeal representation in/and the body politic

1 For example, John Locke *Two Treatises of Government* London: Cambridge University Press, 1967; Jean-Jacques Rousseau *The Social Contract*, Harmondsworth: Penguin, 1968
2 Both Locke and Rousseau held this view. See Locke, *Two Treatises of Government* Book II, Section 82; and Rousseau, *Emile* London: Dent & Sons, 1972, pp. 370, 412, 442
3 Thomas Hobbes *Leviathan* Harmondsworth: Penguin, 1968, pp. 81–2
4 ibid., p. 186
5 See Jane Flax 'Mother-Daughter Relationships: psychodynamics, politics and philosophy' in H. Eisenstein and A. Jardine (eds) *The Future of Difference* Boston: G. K. Hall, 1980, especially p. 29f
6 See C. Pateman *The Sexual Contract* Cambridge: Polity Press, 1988, especially chapter four
7 Mary Wollstonecraft *A Vindication of the Rights of Woman* (1792) Harmondsworth: Penguin, 1975
8 The notion of ethics which I have in mind is one that takes the body, its pleasures, powers and capacities into account. A good example is B. Spinoza's *Ethics*. For an account of what Spinoza's ethical theory can offer us today, see Gilles Deleuze *Spinoza: Practical Philosophy* San Francisco: City Lights Books, 1988, especially chapters two and six.
9 Italo Calvino *Invisible Cities* London: Picador, 1979, p. 39

8: Corpus delicti: the body at the scene of writing

1 Impossible as it may seem, not everyone does find him/herself in possession of a body. See for example, H. Head *Studies in Neurology* Oxford: Oxford University Press, 1920; P. Schilder *The Image and Appearance of the Human Body* New York: International Universities Press, 1950; O. Sacks *The Man Who Mistook His Wife For A Hat* London: Picador, 1985
2 P. Valéry 'Some Simple Reflections on the Body' in M. Feher with R. Naddaff and N. Tazi (eds) *Fragments for a History of the Human Body* Part Two New York: Urzone, 1989, pp. 398–9

3 S. de Beauvoir *The Second Sex* H. M. Parshley (trans.) [orig. 1949] London: Jonathan Cape, 1953, p. 13

4 ibid., p. 273

5 E. Grosz 'A Note on Essentialism and Difference' in S. Gunew (ed.) *Feminist Knowledge: Critique and Construct* London: Routledge, forthcoming

6 ibid.

7 ibid.

8 The 'two lips' refers to the essay 'This Sex Which Is Not One' in L. Irigaray *This Sex Which Is Not One* C. Porter with C. Burke (trans.) Ithaca, New York: Cornell University Press, 1985 pp. 23–33

9 For a useful and concise analysis of the sex/gender distinction see M. Gatens 'A Critique of the Sex/Gender Distinction' in J. Allen and P. Patton (eds) *Beyond Marxism? Interventions After Marx* Sydney: Intervention, 1983, pp. 143–60 and reprinted in S. Gunew (ed.) *A Reader in Feminist Knowledge* London: Routledge (forthcoming)

10 See, for example, S. Heath 'Difference' *Screen* 19:3, Autumn 1978, pp. 50–112; G. C. Spivak 'Displacement And The Discourse Of Woman' in M. Krupnick (ed.) in *Displacement: Derrida and After* Bloomington: Indiana University Press, 1983, pp. 169–95; N. Schor 'Introducing feminism' *Paragraph* 8, 1986, pp. 94–101; N. Schor 'Dreaming Dissymmetry: Barthes, Foucault, and Sexual Difference' in A. Jardine and P. Smith (eds) *Men in Feminism* New York and London: Methuen, 1987, pp. 98–110; N. Schor 'This essentialism which is not one' *Differences* 1: 2, Summer 1989, pp. 38–58; D. J. Fuss '"Essentially Speaking": Luce Irigaray's Language of Essence' *Hypatia* 3:3, Winter 1989, pp. 62–80; A. Jardine 'Men in Feminism: Odor di Uomo Or Compagnons de Route?' in *Men in Feminism* pp. 54–61; R. Braidotti 'The politics of ontological difference' in T. Brennan (ed.) *Between Feminism and Psychoanalysis* London and New York: Routledge, 1989, pp. 89–105; E. Grosz 'A Note on Essentialism and Difference'; C. Vasseleu 'Life itself' in this collection.

11 E. Grosz 'A Note on Essentialism and Difference'

12 ibid.

13 T. Moi *Sexual/Textual Politics: Feminist Literary Theory* London and New York: Routledge, 1988, p. 139

14 E. Grosz 'A Note on Essentialism and Difference'

15 See, for example, T. Moi *Sexual/Textual Politics* pp. 138–9. Moi regards Irigaray's work as tainted because she has presumed to enter discourse as a woman. She mentions Margaret Thatcher to illustrate the folly of a woman entering a man's arena *as* a woman. For inevitably, woman must act as if she were a man and thereby deny the specificity of her difference. Moi cites the battery of questions that Shoshana Felman raises regarding the place of enunciation in Irigaray's '*parler femme*'. And Irigaray stands condemned, with no further argument. Moi seems to have no understanding of the Derridean strategy that levers a text open by attending to the differences that always inhabit it, even as they are finessed and suppressed. She misunderstands Derrida when she refers to his claim that there is no outside of metaphysics, drawing the

conclusion that Irigaray's project is therefore doomed to failure because there is ultimately no escape. Derrida argues from the inside out, trying to articulate an 'inside' of metaphysics where 'the logic of the same' cannot maintain its supposed self-identity. And clearly, Irigaray makes use of this strategy to reread phallogocentrism. Against the philosophical complexity of Irigaray's work, Moi's argument can only work as *ressentiment*. It is as though Moi believes she can escape the question of enunciation in her own work and prove that she is outside the 'Thatcher effect' by pointing to error and guilt elsewhere. We might well ask, from what position does Moi speak?

16 ibid., p. 148

17 D. J. Fuss '"Essentially Speaking"' p. 62

18 Much of Irigaray's writing is still untranslated. Among anglophone readers her better known works include 'Women's Exile' C. Venn (trans.) *Ideology and Consciousness* 1 May 1977, pp. 62–76; *Speculum of the other woman* G. C. Gill (trans.) Ithaca, New York: Cornell University Press, 1985; *This Sex Which Is Not One* C. Porter with C. Burke (trans.) Ithaca, New York: Cornell University Press, 1985; 'Is the Subject of Science Sexed?' E. Oberle (trans.) *Cultural Critique* 1 Fall, 1985, pp. 73–88

19 J. Gallop '*Quand Nos Lèvres S'Écrivent*: Irigaray's Body Politic' *Romanic Review* 74:1, 1983, pp. 77–83. This article appears in a slightly revised version as 'Lip Service' in J. Gallop *Thinking Through The Body* New York: Columbia University Press, 1988, pp. 92–100. I have concentrated on this article because, as D. J. Fuss comments, Jane Gallop is a noted defender of Irigaray and one whose work represents '... the most promising line of argument to follow'. '"Essentially Speaking"' p. 65

20 J. Gallop 'Quand Nos Lèvres S'Écrivent' p. 83

21 ibid., p. 78. By way of defending a too literal reading of Irigaray, it may be that Gallop has engaged in a too literal reading of Freud. Certainly, the provocative ambiguities in Freud's work suggest that other interpretations are also possible.

22 ibid., p. 79

23 ibid., p. 83

24 ibid., p. 81

25 ibid., p. 82

26 ibid., p. 80

27 Gallop is not alone in excluding biology from consideration. There seems to be an almost consensual agreement among Irigaray's most sophisticated defenders that a limit must be determined with regard to the notion of materiality, textuality or anatomy in Irigaray's texts. See, for example, M. Whitford 'Luce Irigaray and the Female Imaginary: Speaking as a Woman' *Radical Philosophy* 43, Summer 1986, p. 7 and 'Rereading Irigaray' in T. Brennan (ed.) *Between Feminism and Psychoanalysis* London and New York: Routledge, 1989, pp. 121–123. Whitford is careful to exclude biology from Irigaray's interventions. 'She (Irigaray) is speaking not of biology but of the *imaginary*, in which one may make male *or* female identifications, regardless of one's biolo-

gical sex.' 1986, p. 7. Biology in this account is immutable; the 'given' of sex that sexuality then interprets.

See also C. Burke 'Irigaray Through The Looking Glass' *Feminist Studies* 7:2, 1981, pp. 303–4. A certain 'play' within Burke's writing tends to sustain the uncertain nature of the body's materiality. Burke suggests that 'the problematic intersection of sexuality and representation' could be thought through an attention to the notion and use of figurative language, a study that has still to be undertaken. This seems to imply that figuration may involve some material efficacy, that it may not be the 'other' of literalisation. Burke goes on to cite Nietzsche who muses as to whether all philosophy 'has not been merely an interpretation of the body and a misunderstanding of the body'. Of course, 'body' is ambiguous here. It could be the subject or the predicate of the sentence, or indeed their performative implication. The mind/body split is made unstable in this statement. This undecidability could be taken as an opening for an investigation of the inextricable nature of language and/as materiality, however Burke confines the ambiguity in the passage between the words 'interpretation' and 'misunderstanding'. This tends to 'read' the body back into a hermeneutic horizon, burying its substance beneath the debris of our understandings or misunderstandings. Consequently, Burke is only able to acknowledge the worth of reinterpreting the 'conceptual' systems through which the body is understood. And although the conclusion to this piece evokes the possibility that reading is an action, that reading enacts differences and therefore has effects, the interpretive model through which this is argued inevitably privileges mind over matter. As Burke suggests, 'we may find that we emerge from this difficult reading process with our minds, literally, changed'.

And see E. Grosz *Sexual Subversions: Three French Feminists* Sydney: Allen & Unwin, 1989, pp. xix–xx. Grosz's discussion of morphology sets up a surface/depth model, a culture/physiology (biology) split. Consequently, the efficacy of Irigaray's '*parler femme*' is confined to the notion of 'inscription' on the body's surface. Anatomy is read as the body's corporeal shape.

My own argument is not in opposition to these excellent readings, and indeed, I am entirely indebted to their intelligent provocations. Rather, I see my intervention as an elaboration or extension of this work. In other words, although I agree with Carolyn Burke that our minds are literally changed, I want to entertain the idea that our bodies are also.

28 See, for example, M. Plaza '"Phallomorphic power" and the psychology of "woman"' *Ideology and Consciousness* 4, Autumn 1978, pp. 57–76; T. Moi *Sexual/Textual Politics* pp. 127–49; E. H. Kuykendall 'Toward an Ethic of Nurturance: Luce Irigaray on Mothering and Power' in J. Trebilcot (ed.) *Mothering: Essays in Feminist Theory* Totowa N. J.: Rowman & Allanheld, 1984, pp. 263–74; J. Sayers *Sexual Contradictions: Psychology, Psychoanalysis, and Feminism* London: Tavistock, 1986, pp. 42–8

29 J. Gallop 'Quand Nos Lèvres S'Écrivent' p. 79

30 See, for example, 'The function and field of speech and language in psychoanalysis' in J. Lacan *Écrits* A. Sheridan (trans.) New York, London: W W Norton, 1977, pp. 30–113. Liz Grosz has suggested to me that perhaps a radical reading of Lacan's mirror stage could go towards generalising Lacan's field of language. Such an interpretation would offer an interesting and suggestive line of inquiry.

31 A glaring illustration of this tendency to ignore a Derridean notion of 'writing', 'language' or 'textuality' is evidenced in J. Gallop '*Writing and Sexual Difference*: The Difference Within' in E. Abel (ed.) *Writing and Sexual Difference* Brighton, Sussex: The Harvester Press, 1982, pp. 283–90. Gallop's intervention fastens onto an oversight or blind spot in the collection; the inability to take account of what Barbara Johnson describes as 'not a difference between ... but a difference within. Far from constituting the text's unique identity, it is that which subverts the very idea of identity'. Johnson describes this as a 'literature that inhabits the very heart of what makes sexuality problematic for us speaking animals.' p. 284. Gallop quickly assumes that 'Johnson's puzzling remark could best be explained by recourse to Lacanian psychoanalysis', although she does go on to admit that 'my attempt to explain Johnson's provocative remark is far from satisfactory' p. 285. It seems strange that Gallop has chosen to ignore the original context in which Johnson's apparently enigmatic words appeared, *The Critical Difference: Essays in the Contemporary Rhetoric of Reading* Baltimore and London: Johns Hopkins University Press, 1980. Johnson is quite specific in describing that volume as a working through of a Derridean notion of *différance*, 'the record of one reader's struggles to come to grips with the problems posed by contemporary so-called deconstructive critical theory' p. xi. When Gallop confines this enterprise to the problematic of a psychoanalytic narrative, a 'critical difference' is elided.

32 Several critics have noted the way that Derrida's work has received a sanitising translation as it crossed the Atlantic. See, for example, R. Gasché 'Deconstruction as Criticism' *Glyph* 6, pp. 177–215; B. Johnson, 'Taking Fidelity Philosophically' in J. F. Graham (ed.) *Difference in Translation* Ithaca and London: Cornell University Press, 1985, pp. 142–48; G. C. Spivak 'Marx After Derrida' in W. E. Cain (ed.) *Philosophical Approaches to Literature: New Essays on Nineteenth and Twentieth Century Texts* Lewisburg: Bucknell University Press, 1984, pp. 227–52; S. Weber *Institution and Interpretation* Minneapolis: University of Minnesota Press, 1987.

33 See J. Derrida 'Freud and the Scene of Writing' in *Writing And Difference* A. Bass (trans.) London: Routledge & Kegan Paul, 1985. It struck me that the title of Gallop's article 'Quand Nos Lèvres S'Écrivent', a play on Irigaray's 'Quand nos lèvres se parlent' could be read through the circuit of the mystic writing pad. The reflexive casts an ambiguity that has the lips being written at the same time as they are writing themselves.

34 S. Kofman as quoted in A. Jardine *Gynesis: Configurations of Woman and Modernity* Ithaca and London: Cornell University Press, 1985, p. 182

35 As the notion of the 'play' within writing has been so consistently misinterpreted, it is worth quoting Derrida himself on this word: 'Play, not in the sense of gambling or playing games, but what in French we call *jouer*, which means that the structure of the machine, or the springs, are not so tight, so that you can just try to dislocate; that's what I meant by play.' As quoted in R. Ferrel 'Xenophobia: At the border of philosophy and literature', R. Freadman and L. Reinhardt (eds) *On Literary Theory & Philosophy: A Cross-disciplinary Encounter*, London: Macmillan, forthcoming

36 Irigaray has often been taken to task over her cryptic comment, 'I think we must go back to the question not of the anatomy but of the morphology of the female sex.' 'Women's Exile' p. 64. See, for example, T. Moi *Sexual/Textual Politics* p. 143; D. J. Fuss '"Essentially Speaking"' p. 77; M. Plaza '"Phallomorphic power" and the psychology of "woman"' p. 31. A more complex understanding of morphology, one enabled by a deconstructive reading, would not be so puzzled by Irigaray's comment. Although, having said this, I am not assuming that this interpretation is necessarily Irigaray's. Rather, my own intention here is to offer what might be a more useful reading of this problematic. I would like to acknowledge that my interpretation of morphology derives from material studied in a seminar given by Gayatri Spivak, 'Theory, Feminism, Marxism and the Third World', Stanford, Spring 1988.

37 I am trying to think Michel Foucault's 'how' of power, which enacts the materiality of inscription, together with Derrida's political economy of 'value' as 'writing in the general sense'.

38 On the question of the referent, Derrida has often been accused of abandoning reference together. However, he insists that: 'It is totally false to suggest that deconstruction is a suspension of reference ... deconstruction tries to show that the question of reference is much more complex and problematic than traditional theories supposed.' See 'Deconstruction and the other: An interview with Richard Kearney' in R. Kearney (ed.) *Dialogues with contemporary Continental thinkers: The phenomenological heritage* Manchester: Manchester University Press, 1984, p. 123

39 See J. Derrida 'The Supplement of Copula: Philosophy before Linguistics' in *Margins of Philosophy* A. Bass (trans.) Chicago: University of Chicago Press, 1982, pp. 175–205

40 For an example of this tendency, see B. Johnson 'Metaphor, metonymy and voice in H. L. Gates Jr (ed.) in *Their Eyes Were Watching God*' in *Black Literature And Literary Theory* New York and London: Methuen, 1984, pp. 205–19

41 G. Spivak 'Displacement And The Discourse Of Woman' p. 191

42 See J. Derrida 'Différance' in *Margins of Philosophy* pp. 1–27

43 See J. Derrida *Spurs: Nietzsche's Styles* B. Harlow (trans.) Chicago and London: University of Chicago Press, 1979

44 G. C. Spivak 'Feminism and deconstruction, again: negotiating with unacknowledged masculism' in *Between Feminism and Psychoanalysis* p. 220

45 V. Kirby 'Corporeographies' *Inscriptions: Journal for the Critique of Colonial Discourse* 5, UCSC, 1989, pp. 103–119

9: The advent of America at EPCOT Center

1 Henry Adams *The Education of Henry Adams* in *Novels, Mont Saint Michel, The Education* New York: Library of America, 1983, p. 1145. Adams' *Education* (1907), an autobiography written in the third person, may be unfamiliar to Australian readers. Suffice to say that, especially in its final chapters, it turns on Adams' recognition that his enlightenment heritage (from forbears Presidents John and John Quincy Adams) has left him utterly unprepared to consider a world moulded by the forces that enlightenment science and industry have unleashed. He conceives of this problematic in terms of the Virgin and the Dynamo, which stand for the old and new forces that have propelled the West.

2 Adams, p. 1147

3 Umberto Eco *Travels in Hyperreality* William Weaver (trans.) Orlando: Harcourt, Brace, Jovanovich, 1986, p. 292

4 There are, in fact, a small number of responsibly curated, authentic, cultural 'treasures' exhibited in some of the 'countries' of the World Showcase, but these are peripheral and discreetly marked. As far as technology goes, very little machinery is on display. Rather, the workings of machinery are represented by other kinds of machines.

5 Eco, p. 299

6 The Walt Disney Company *EPCOT Center Guide Book*, 1989. Further quotations are from this publication unless otherwise noted.

7 The juxtaposition of cultural and futuristic/technological content has been fairly standard since the 1939 New York World's Fair. In fact, the plan of EPCOT is quite similar to that of the 1939 Fair.

8 Mainstreet USA is an approximately 5/8 scale 'reproduction' of Walt Disney's childhood 'hometown' (or one of them—his family moved a lot), and the slightly toylike, unreal quality of the architecture seems to be very important to its success. On Mainstreet USA and its function in the context of Disneyland/The Magic Kingdom, see Louis Marin *Utoppics, Spatial Play* Robert Vollrath (trans.) New York: Humanities Press, 1984, pp. 239–57 and Eco 'Travels in Hyperreality' pp. 39–48

9 The Venetian locale only 'works' as a vista from the pathway around the lagoon. Once you walk into Italy's 'piazza', you discover that Venice is juxtaposed with various Roman baroque elements.

10 The reasons for this are discussed in Richard Francaviglia 'Main Street USA: A Comparison/Contrast of Streetscapes in Disneyland and Walt Disney World' *Journal of Popular Culture* 15,1, Summer 1981. Francaviglia's ideas are expanded upon in relation to shopping malls in 'Mousekatecture on Main Street', Chapter 6 of William Severini Kowinski *The Malling of America* New York: William Morrow, 1985. These analyses of Main Street USA improve on Marin's in several respects. Most notably, they give considerably more attention to the possibilities for pleasure in sanitised simulacra of public space.

11 This should not be taken as a criticism of de Certeau (though Disney World certainly presents problems he didn't consider). Indeed, De Cer-

teau would reply that any attempt to account for a highly systematic 'strategy' like EPCOT Center is necessarily going to fail to account for its 'tactical' residuals. Thus, though the strategic groundplan of EPCOT is my visible concern in this essay, it is the possibility of a tactics, of a way of 'poaching' Disney World, that allows the rethinking of the reception of EPCOT that I'm attempting in this essay. Put in De Certeau's terms, my suggestion here is that EPCOT's strategic effort to anticipate tactical and narrative procedures pushes it just a little beyond homology and opens the possibility for certain kinds of tactical procedures. See Michel de Certeau *The Practice of Everyday Life* Steven Rendall (trans.) Berkeley: UC Press, 1984, especially chapters V and VII.

12 Sadly, this effect has been tainted by the construction, between France and the UK, of a huge new hotel complex designed by postmodernist architect Michael Graves, which adds two colossal dolphins and a colossal swan to the Showcase panorama, with predictably surreal effects.

13 This figure is quoted in Richard Schickel *The Disney Version: The Life, Times, Art and Commerce of Walt Disney* rev. edn, New York: Simon & Schuster, 1985, p. 398. Schickel's book also contains some thoughtful observations on Disneyland (pp. 295–337) which reinforce my interpretation of the reception of Disney's 'imagineering' exhibits.

14 In contrast to the unified family of 'Horizons', a central moment in 'The American Adventure' is the division of a family, by which the exhibit tells the story of the Civil War.

15 Strikingly absent from this inventory is the typically 'postmodern' vision of the future, the gritty, dysptopic future of films like *Blade Runner*. This chronotope which is often interpreted as (to use Jameson's term) 'post-millenarian' or post-apocalyptic, is represented at EPCOT only in the 3–D film *Captain Eo*, starring Michael Jackson. Its absence marks Future World as a sort of monument to the modernist vision it endlessly replays. Precisely because of the degree of repetition, though, the whole of Future World can itself be viewed as a kind of post-apocalyptic museum. On the post-millenarian chronotope see Vivian Sobchack *Screening Space: The American Science Fiction Film* New York: Ungar Publishing, 1987, Chapter 4.

16 I am thinking particularly of Marin, although his rather heavy-handed analyses of the ideological content of Disneyland (e.g. its undoubted validations of the history of imperialist domination) can, I think, be separated from his very subtle analyses of the park's rituals of entry and of the ways in which the Park's design helps induce the personal narrative of consumption.

17 The idea of a graphic or cinematographic literacy that I suggest here picks up on some themes from media theory as it influenced the 'pop' movement of the 1960s, on which see Reyner Banham *Design by Choice* Penny Sparke (ed.) New York: Rizzoli, 1981, especially 'Who Is this "Pop"?', 'The Triumph of Software', and 'Summa Galactica'.

18 'Behold, the glory of the Sistine ceiling!' says Walter, without any sort of preparation or explanation, and since we are in the realm of the cinematographic here, Michelangelo/Charlton Heston paints Spaceship

Earth on his back, even though the evidence is perfectly clear that the Sistine ceiling was painted from a standing position.

19 The absolution that occurs in Spaceship Earth might be thought of as a singularity. This word refers to a mathematically indeterminable point, such as that out of which some physicists imagine the universe to have expanded. It also has acquired two other meanings, both of which are relevant in this context. In reference to black holes, the singularity is the boundary beyond which the gravity of the (inferred) black hole is so great that even light cannot bounce out of it, which means that nothing can be determined about it. 'The Singularity' has also been used recently to name the ideal information state (invoked in Spaceship Earth by AT & T and by Lyotard in his 'report on knowledge') of hypertextuality, in which, more or less, all information would be equally available for use by everybody. According to the theorists of 'The Singularity', the achievement of this state will result in changes in human consciousness so far-reaching that they simply cannot be predicted. See the seminal manifesto: Marc Stiegler 'Hypermedia and the Singularity' *Analog Science Fiction/Science Fact*, Nov. 1988.

10: Business, pleasure, narrative: The folktale in our times

1 André Amar 'A Psychoanalytic Study of Money' Ernest Borneman (ed.) *The Psychoanalysis of Money* New York: Urizen Books, 1976, p. 283

2 For an instance of the contemporary return of anxieties relating to the handling of money, and in particular the anti-Semitism attached to it, see Connie Bruck *The Predators' Ball: The Junk Bond Raiders and the Man who Staked Them* New York: Simon & Schuster, 1988. This book deals with the rise of the US merchant bank, Drexel, Burnham Lambert and in particular its junk bond specialist, Michael Milken.

3 The best known of these is of course Marx's *Capital*. Less well known, but of considerable use to us because of its aesthetic emphasis is George Simmel's *The Philosophy of Money* Tom Bottomore and David Frisby (trans.) London: Routledge & Kegan Paul, 1978

4 Milton Friedman in the preface to *The Optimum Quantity of Money and Other Essays* Chicago: Aldine Publishing, 1969

5 Martin Shubik *Games for Society, Business and War: Towards a Theory of Gaming* Amsterdam: Elsevier Scientific Publishing, 1976, p. 60. For a much more interesting and more rigorous account of claims like this see Ian Hacking *The Emergence of Probability: A Philosophical Study of Early Ideas about Probability, Induction, and Statistical Inference* Cambridge: Cambridge University Press, 1975

6 Michel Foucault 'The Prose of the World' in *The Order of Things: An Archaeology of the Human Sciences*, New York: Vintage Books, 1973, p. 17

7 'The "threat" of corporate debt'; editorial, *Sydney Morning Herald*, 1 February 1990

8 Quoted by I. A. Richards in *The Philosophy of Rhetoric* Oxford: Oxford University Press, 1936, p. 6

9 V. Propp, *Morphology of the Folk Tale* Austin: University of Texas, 1975

10 For example, Carol Austin, on the "Carleton-Walsh Report" on the ABC, and Glenda Korporaal, on the Sunday morning business program on Channel 10, which Walsh hosted. Curiously, Sunday morning business programs have begun to disappear, so perhaps the moment of fascination with money has passed, along with the entrepreneurs, whose lives have been relegated to the status of last year's top rating soapies.

11 Propp, p. 79

12 *Sydney Morning Herald* 19 February 1990, p. 29

13 ibid.

Notes on contributors

Geoffrey Batchen has degrees in architecture and fine art, and has worked extensively in the visual arts industry, including for art museums and curating exhibitions shown in Australia, US and Brazil. His many published articles include pieces in *Afterimage, History of Photography* and *Photofile.* In 1983–84 he was a Rubinstein Fellow with the Whitney Museum of American Art in New York.

Jennifer Biddle has degrees in linguistics and anthropology. She currently lives in Lajamanu in the Northern Territory, where she endeavours to learn something of the many forms of Warlpiri writing. Her work on the effects of translation is supported by grants from the Australian Institute of Aboriginal Studies and the Department of Anthropology, University of Sydney.

Rosalyn Diprose has degrees in biomedical science and philosophy and her various published papers include pieces in *Radical Philosophy* and *Australian Feminist Studies.* She has taught at the University of New South Wales and Sydney University and her research on ethics, embodiment and sexual difference has been supported by a fellowship from the American Association of University Women, held at the University of California.

Robyn Ferrell is the author of a novel *The Weather and Other Gods* as well as several academic articles on philosophy, literature and psychoanalysis. She has worked as a journalist on the *Sydney Morning Herald*, and now teaches philosophy at the University of New South Wales.

Moira Gatens teaches philosophy at the Australian National University and is the author of *Feminism and Philosophy* (Polity Press, Cambridge, 1990) and articles in journals and collections including in *Australian Feminist Studies* and *The Australasian Journal of Philosophy.* She is currently writing a book on ethics and philosophies of the body.

Helen Grace is a photographer and film-maker, known for *Serious Undertakings*. She is the editor of the interdisciplinary journal *West*, and teaches art history at the University of Western Sydney (Nepean). She is published in *Cultural Studies*, *Art & Text* and *Photofile* and is currently working on a monograph on the Australian artist Susan Norrie.

Vicki Kirby is published in diverse journals including *Australian Feminist Studies*, *Mankind*, *Inscriptions* and *Art & Text*. She has held a fellowship from the American Association of University Women, at the University of California Santa Cruz and Stanford University. She has degrees in literature and anthropology and a diploma of education and is working on deconstruction, feminism and cultural difference.

Paul Patton has degrees from Sydney University and the University of Paris VIII, and is currently translating Gilles Deleuze's *Difference et Repetition* for Athlone Press. He teaches aesthetics, Nietzsche and contemporary French philosophy at the Australian National University. His many publications include a recent article on Foucault in *Political Studies*.

Steve Rugare has a degree in political theory from Michigan State University and is currently studying in the History of Consciousness program at the University of California, Santa Cruz. His interests include history and theory of architecture, phenomenology, hermeneutics and opera.

Cathryn Vasseleu's published articles include pieces in *The Illusion of Life* (Power Institute, Sydney, 1990) papers on animation and in *West*. She has degrees in philosophy and biomedical science and is working in the area of vision and embodiment in the Department of General Philosophy at Sydney University. She is currently also making an animated film on conception.

Select bibliography

Adams, Henry *Novels, Mont Saint Michel, The Education* New York: Library of America, 1983

Ainley, Alison '"Ideal Selfishness"—Nietzsche's Metaphor of Modernity' D. F. Krell and D. Wood (eds) *Exceedingly Nietzsche* London: Routledge, 1988

Amar, André 'A Psychoanalytic Study of Money' Ernest Borneman (ed.) *The Psychoanalysis of Money* New York: Urizen Books, 1976

Anderson, Christopher and Françoise Dussart 'Dreamings in Acrylic: Western Desert Art' in Peter Sutton (ed.) *Dreamings: The Art of Aboriginal Australia* New York and Adelaide: Viking in assoc. with The Asia Society Galleries and Penguin Books, 1988, pp. 89–142

Bachelard, Gaston *The Psychoanalysis of Fire* (1938) Alan C. M. Ross (trans.) London and New York: Quartet Books, 1987

Banham, Reyner *Design by Choice* Penny Sparke (ed.) New York: Rizzoli, 1981

Barthes, Roland *Image, Music, Text* Stephen Heath (trans.) New York: Hill & Wang, 1977

Batchen, Geoffrey 'Photography, Power and Representation' *Afterimage* 16:4, Nov. 1988, pp. 7–9

de Beauvoir, Simone *The Second Sex* (1949) H. M. Parshley (trans.) London: Jonathan Cape, 1953

Benjamin, Walter *Illuminations* Hannah Arendt (ed.) Harry Zohn (trans.) New York: Schocken Books, 1969

Berman, Marshall *All That is Solid Melts Into Air* New York: Simon & Schuster, 1982

Bernstein, Richard 'One Step Forward, Two Steps Backward: Richard Rorty on Liberal Democracy and Philosophy' *Political Theory* 15:4, 1987, pp. 538–63

Braidotti, Rosi 'The Politics of Ontological Difference' Teresa Brennan (ed.) *Between Feminism and Psychoanalysis* London and New York: Routledge, 1989

Brennan, Teresa (ed.) *Between Feminism and Psychoanalysis* London and New York: Routledge, 1989
Burke, Caroline 'Irigaray Through the Looking Glass' *Feminist Studies* 7:2, 1981, pp. 303–4
Canetti, Elias *Crowds and Power* Carol Stewart (trans.) Harmondsworth: Penguin, 1973
de Certeau, Michel *The Practice of Everyday Life* Steven Rendell (trans.) Berkeley: University of California Press, 1984
Clifford, James and George E. Marcus *Writing Culture: the poetics and politics of ethnography* Berkeley: University of California Press, 1986
Deleuze, Gilles 'Plato and the Simulacrum' Rosalind Krauss (trans.) *October* 27, Winter 1983, pp. 47–56
——*Spinoza: Practical Philosophy* (1970) Robert Hurley (trans.) San Francisco: City Lights Books, 1988
Deleuze, Gilles and Felix Guattari *Anti-Oedipus: Capitalism and Schizophrenia* (1972) Robert Hurley, Mark Seem and Helen R. Lane (trans.) Minneapolis: University of Minnesota Press, 1983
——*A Thousand Plateaus: Capitalism and Schizophrenia* (1980) Brian Massumi (trans.) Minneapolis: University of Minnesota Press, 1987
Derrida, Jacques *Edmund Husserl's Origin of Geometry: An Introduction* (1962) John P. Leavey Jr (trans.) Lincoln and London: University of Nebraska Press, 1989
——*Of Grammatology* (1967) Gayatri Spivak (trans.) Baltimore: Johns Hopkins University Press, 1976
——*Writing and Difference* (1967) Alan Bass (trans.) Chicago: University of Chicago Press, 1978; London and Henley: Routledge & Kegan Paul, 1978
——*Margins of Philosophy* (1972) Alan Bass (trans.) Chicago: University of Chicago Press, 1982
——*Positions* (1972) Alan Bass (trans.) Chicago: University of Chicago Press, 1972
——*Spurs: Nietzsche's Styles* (1976) Barbara Harlow (trans.) Chicago and London: University of Chicago Press, 1979, Bilingual edition
Diprose, Rosalyn 'Nietzsche, Ethics and Sexual Difference' *Radical Philosophy* 52, 1989 pp. 27–33
Diprose, Rosalyn and Cathy Vasseleu, 'Animation–AIDS and Science/Fiction' A. Cholodenko (ed.) *The Illusion of Life* Sydney: The Power Institute, 1990
Eco, Umberto *Travels in Hyperreality* William Weaver (trans.) Orlando: Harcourt, Brace, Jovanovich, 1986
Farley, John *Gametes and Spores* Baltimore and London: Johns Hopkins University Press, 1982
Ferrell, Robyn 'Life-Threatening Life: Angela Carter and the Uncanny' in *The Illusion of Life* Sydney: The Power Institute, 1990
——'Xenophobia: At the Border of Philosophy and Literature' in Richard Freadman and Lloyd Reinhardt (eds) *On Literary Theory and Philosophy: A Cross-disciplinary Encounter* London: Macmillan, forthcoming
Flax, Jane 'Mother-Daughter Relationships: Psychodynamics, Politics and

Philosophy' H. Eisenstein and A. Jardine (eds) *The Future of Difference* Boston: G.K. Hall, 1980

Foucault, Michel *The Birth of The Clinic: An Archaeology of Medical Perception* (1963) A.M. Sheridan Smith (trans.) New York: Vintage/Random House, 1975

——*The Archaeology of Knowledge* (1969) A.M. Sheridan Smith (trans.) New York: Pantheon Books, 1972

——*The Order of Things: An Archaeology of the Human Sciences* (1970) New York: Vintage/Random House, 1973

——*The History of Sexuality Volume I* (1976) Robert Hurley (trans.) New York: Vintage/Random House, 1978

——*Language, Counter-Memory, Practice* Donald F. Bouchard (ed.) Ithaca, New York: Cornell University Press, 1977

——*Discipline and Punish: The Birth of the Prison* (1975) Alan Sheridan (trans.) Harmondsworth: Penguin, 1977

——*Power/Knowledge: Selected Interviews and Other Writings 1972–1977* Colin Gordon (ed.) Brighton: Harvester Press, 1980

——*The Use of Pleasure: The History of Sexuality Volume Two* (1984) Robert Hurley (trans.) New York: Vintage/Random House, 1985

Francaviglia, Richard 'Main Street USA: A Comparison/Contrast of Streetscapes in Disneyland and Walt Disney World' *Journal of Popular Culture* 15:1, 1981

Fuss, Diana J. '"Essentially Speaking": Luce Irigaray's Language of Essence' *Hypatia* 3:3, Winter 1989, pp. 62–80

Gallop, Jane '*Writing and Sexual Difference*: The Difference Within' E. Abel (ed.) *Writing and Sexual Difference* Brighton, Sussex: Harvester Press, 1982

——'*Quand Nos Lèvres S'Ècrivent*: Irigaray's Body Politic' *Romanic Review* 74:1, 1983, pp. 77–83

——*Thinking Through the Body* New York: Columbia University Press, 1988

Gatens, Moira 'A Critique of the Sex/Gender Distinction' Judith Allen and Paul Patton (eds) *Beyond Marxism? Interventions After Marx* Sydney: Intervention, 1983 and reprinted in S. Gunew (ed.) *A Reader in Feminist Knowledge*. London: Routledge (forthcoming)

——'Woman and Her Double(s): Sex, Gender and Ethics' *Australian Feminist Studies* 10, 1989

Grosz, Elizabeth *Sexual Subversions: Three French Feminists* Sydney: Allen & Unwin, 1989

——'A Note on Essentialism and Difference' S. Gunew (ed.) *Feminist Knowledge: Critique and Construct* London: Routledge (forthcoming)

Gunning, Tom 'An Aesthetic of Astonishment: Early Film and the (In)credulous Spectator' *Art and Text* 34, Spring 1989, pp. 31–45

Haraway, Donna 'The Biopolitics of Postmodern Bodies: Determinations of Self in Immune System Discourse' *Differences* 1:1, 1989, pp. 2–43

Heidegger, Martin *Being and Time* (1927) John Macquarie and Edward Robinson (trans.) New York: Harper & Row, 1962

Hobbes, Thomas *Leviathan* (1651) Harmondsworth: Penguin, 1968

Irigaray, Luce *Speculum of the Other Woman* (1974) Gillian C. Gill (trans.) Ithaca, New York: Cornell University Press, 1985
——*This Sex Which is Not One* (1977) Catherine Porter and Carolyn Burke (trans.) Ithaca, New York: Cornell University Press, 1985
Johnson, Barbara *The Critical Difference: Essays in the Contemporary Rhetoric of Reading* Baltimore and London: Johns Hopkins Press, 1980
Kirby, Vicki 'Corporeographies' *Inscriptions: Journal for the Critique of Colonial Discourse* 5, 1989, pp. 103–19 (reprinted in *West* 1:1, 1989 pp. 8–11)
de Lauretis, Teresa *Alice Doesn't: Feminism, Semiotics, Cinema* Bloomington: Indiana University Press, 1984
——*Technologies of Gender: Essays on Theory, Film and Fiction* London: MacMillan, 1987
Levinas, Emmanuel *Totality and Infinity* (1961) Alphonso Lingis (trans.) Pittsburgh: Duquesne University Press, 1969
——*Ethics and Infinity: Conversations with Philippe Nemo* (1982) Richard A. Cohen (trans.) Pittsburgh: Duquesne University Press, 1985
Lloyd, Genevieve *The Man of Reason: 'Male' and 'Female' in Western Philosophy* London: Methuen, 1984
Locke, John *Two Treatises of Government* London: Cambridge University Press, 1967
de Man, Paul 'Conclusions: Walter Benjamin's "The Task of the Translator", Messenger Lecture, Cornell University, March 4, 1983' *Yale French Studies* 69, 1985, pp. 25–46
Marin, Louis *Utopics, Spatial Play* Robert Vollrath (trans.) New York: Humanities Press, 1984
Merleau-Ponty, M. *Phenomenology of Perception* Colin Smith (trans.) London: Routledge & Kegan Paul, 1962
Michaels, Eric 'Aboriginal Media History: An Inverted Sequence' unpublished, 1986
——'Western Desert Sandpainting and Postmodernism' in Warlukurlangu Artists *Kuruwarri: Yuendumu Doors* Canberra: Australian Institute of Aboriginal Studies, 1987, pp. 135–43
Moi, Toril *Sexual/Textual Politics: Feminist Literary Theory* London and New York: Routledge, 1988
Muecke, Stephen 'Body, Inscription, Epistemology: Knowing Aboriginal Texts' E. S. Nelson (ed.) *Connections* Canberra: Australian Institute of Aboriginal Studies, 1988, pp. 41–52
Munn, N. D. *Walbiri Iconography: Graphic Representation and Cultural Symbolism in a Central Australian Society* Ithaca and London: Cornell University Press, 1973
——'The Transformation of Subjects into Objects in Walbiri and Pitjantjatjara Myth' in M. Charlesworth (ed.) *Religion in Aboriginal Australia: An Anthology* St Lucia: University of Queensland Press, 1984
Nehamas, Alexander *Nietzsche: Life as Literature* Cambridge, Massachusetts: Harvard University Press, 1985
Newhall, Beaumont *Latent Image: The Discovery of Photography* Albuquerque: University of New Mexico Press, 1967
——*Photography: Essays and Images* London: Secker & Warburg, 1980

Nietzsche, Friedrich *The Birth of Tragedy and the Case of Wagner* (1872) Walter Kaufmann (trans.) New York: Vintage/Random House, 1967

——*Untimely Meditations* (1873–1876) R. J. Hollingdale (trans.) Cambridge: Cambridge University Press, 1983

——*Daybreak* (1881) R. J. Hollingdale (trans.) Cambridge: Cambridge University Press, 1982

——*The Gay Science* (1882) Walter Kaufmann (trans.) New York: Vintage/ Random House, 1974

——*Thus Spoke Zarathustra* (1883–1885) R. J. Hollingdale (trans.) Harmondsworth: Penguin, 1961

——*Beyond Good and Evil* (1886) R. J. Hollingdale (trans.) Harmondsworth: Penguin, 1973

——*On the Genealogy of Morals/Ecce Homo* (1887/1901) Walter Kaufmann and R. J. Hollingdale (trans.) New York: Vintage/Random House, 1967

——*The Will to Power* (1901) Walter Kaufmann and R. J. Hollingdale (trans.) New York: Vintage/Random House, 1968

Norris, Christopher 'Postmodernising History: Right Wing Revisionism and the Uses of Theory' *Southern Review* 21:2, 1988

——'Philosophy as *Not* Just a "Kind of Writing": Derrida and the Claim of Reason' Reed Way Dasenbrock (ed.) *Redrawing the Lines: Analytic Philosophy Deconstruction and Literary Theory*, Minneapolis: University of Minnesota Press, 1989

Pateman, Carole *The Sexual Contract* Cambridge: Polity Press, 1989

Patton, Paul 'Notes for a glossary' *Ideology and Consciousness* 8, 1981, pp. 41–8

——'Taylor and Foucault on Power and Freedom' *Political Studies* 37: 2, 1989, pp. 260–76

Peirce, Charles Sanders *The Writings of Charles S. Peirce: a Chronological Edition* Bloomington: Indiana University Press, 1982

Propp, Vladimir *Morphology of the Folk Tale* (1928) Austin: University of Texas, 1975

Richards, I. A. *The Philosophy of Rhetoric* Oxford: Oxford University Press, 1936

Rorty, Richard *Consequences of Pragmatism* Minneapolis: University of Minnesota Press, 1982

——'Deconstruction and Circumvention' *Critical Inquiry* 11, 1984, pp. 1–23

——'Is Derrida a Transcendental Philosopher?' *Yale Journal of Criticism* 2:2, 1989, pp. 207–18

——'Two Meanings of Logocentrism: A Reply to Norris' Reed Way Dasenbrock (ed.) *Redrawing the Lines: Analytic Philosophy, Deconstruction, and Literary Theory*, Minneapolis: University of Minnesota Press, 1989

——*Contingency, Irony and Solidarity* Cambridge: Cambridge University Press, 1989

Rousseau, Jean-Jacques *The Social Contract* Maurice Cranston (trans.) Harmondsworth: Penguin, 1968

Schenck, David 'The Texture of Embodiment: Foundation for Medical Ethics' *Human Studies* 9, 1989, pp. 43–54

Schickel, Richard *The Disney Version: The Life, Times, Art and Commerce of Walt Disney* (revised edition) New York: Simon & Schuster, 1985

Scott, Charles 'Heidegger and the Question of Ethics' *Research in Phenomenology* 18, 1988, pp. 23–40

Searle, John *Expression and Meaning* Cambridge: Cambridge University Press, 1979

Simmel, George *The Philosophy of Money* Tom Bottomore and David Frisby (trans.) London: Routledge & Kegan Paul, 1978

Spinoza, Benedict 'Ethics' *The Collected Works of Spinoza Vol.I* E. Curley (ed.) Princeton: Princeton University Press, 1985

Spivak, Gayatri Chakravorty 'Displacement and the Discourse of Woman' M. Krupnick (ed.) *Displacement: Derrida and After* Bloomington: Indiana University Press, 1983, pp. 169–95

——'Feminism and deconstruction, again: negotiating with unacknowledged masculinism' Teresa Brennen (ed.) *Between Feminism and Psychoanalysis* London and New York: Routledge, 1989

von Sturmer, John 'Review of P. Roe Gularabulu: Stories from the West Kimberley and B. Shaw Banggaiyerri: The Story of Jack Sullivan as told to Bruce Shaw' *Mankind* 15, 1985, pp. 263–6

——'Aborigines, Representation, Necrophilia' *Art and Text* 32, Autumn 1989, pp. 127–39

Suzuki, David and Knudtson, Peter *Genethics: the Ethics of Engineering Life* Toronto: Stoddart, 1988 and Sydney: Allen & Unwin, 1989

Warlukurlangu Artists *Kuruwarri: Yuendumu Doors* Canberra: Australian Institute of Aboriginal Studies, 1987

Weber, Samuel 'It' *Glyph* 4, 1978, pp. 1–31

——*Institution and Interpretation* Minneapolis: University of Minnesota Press, 1987

Whitford, Margaret 'Luce Irigaray and the Female Imaginary: Speaking as a Woman' *Radical Philosophy* 43, Summer, 1986

——'Rereading Irigaray' Teresa Brennen (ed.) *Between Feminism and Psychoanalysis* London and New York: Routledge, 1989

Wollstonecraft, Mary *A Vindication of the Rights of Woman* (1792) Harmondsworth: Penguin, 1975

Select name index